# Vintage Automobiles

## The Rumble of the Road

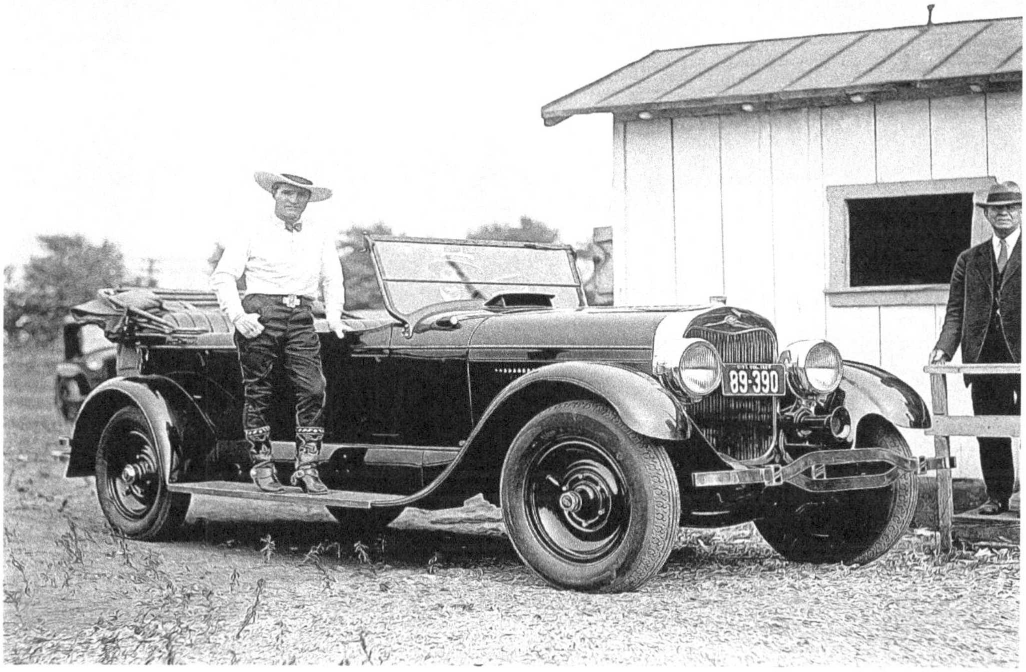

**R.D. Jentsch**



ISBN 978-1517012045

Dedicated to
All the coloring enthusiasts
My Family
My Best Friend
&
All the Drama

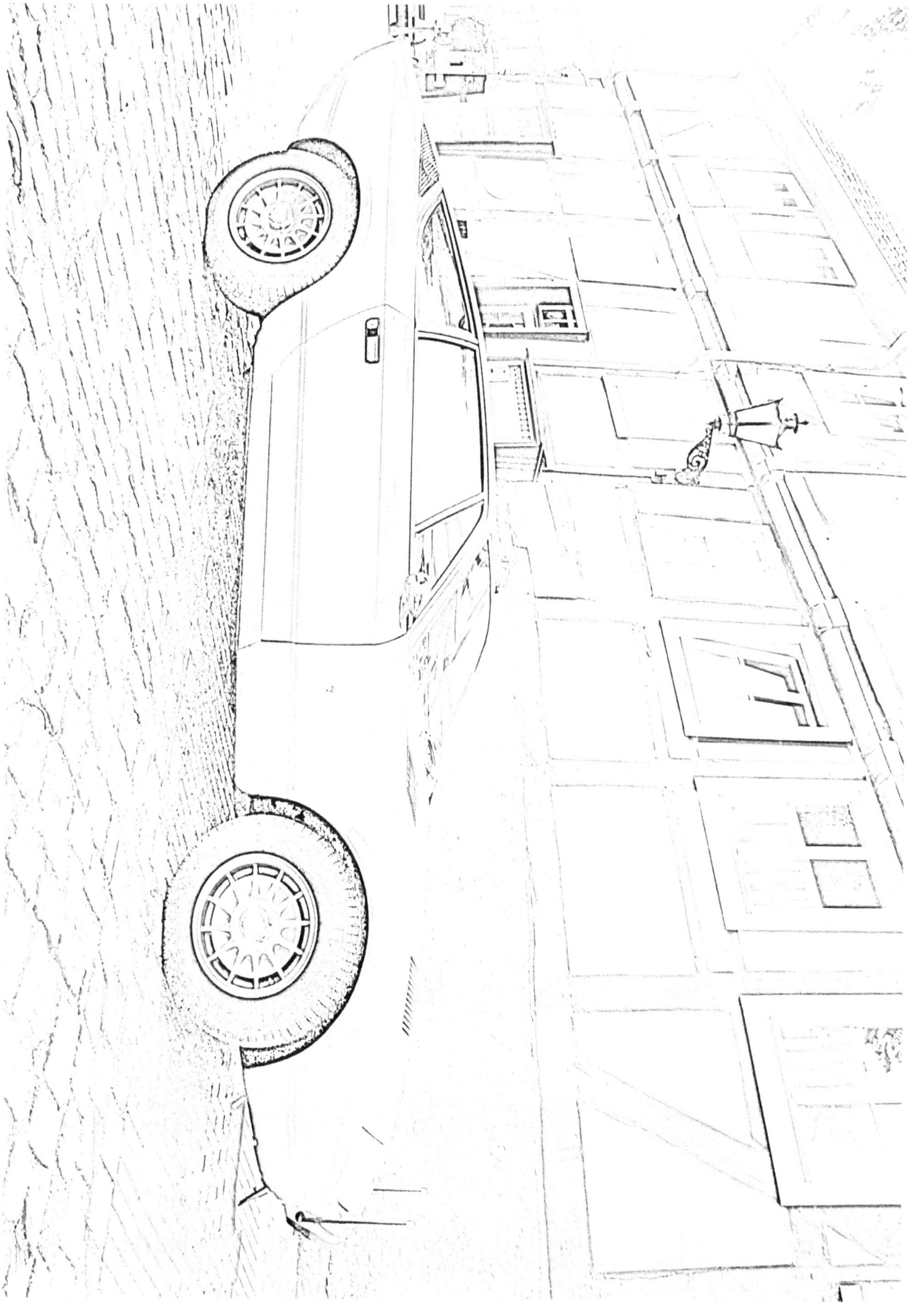

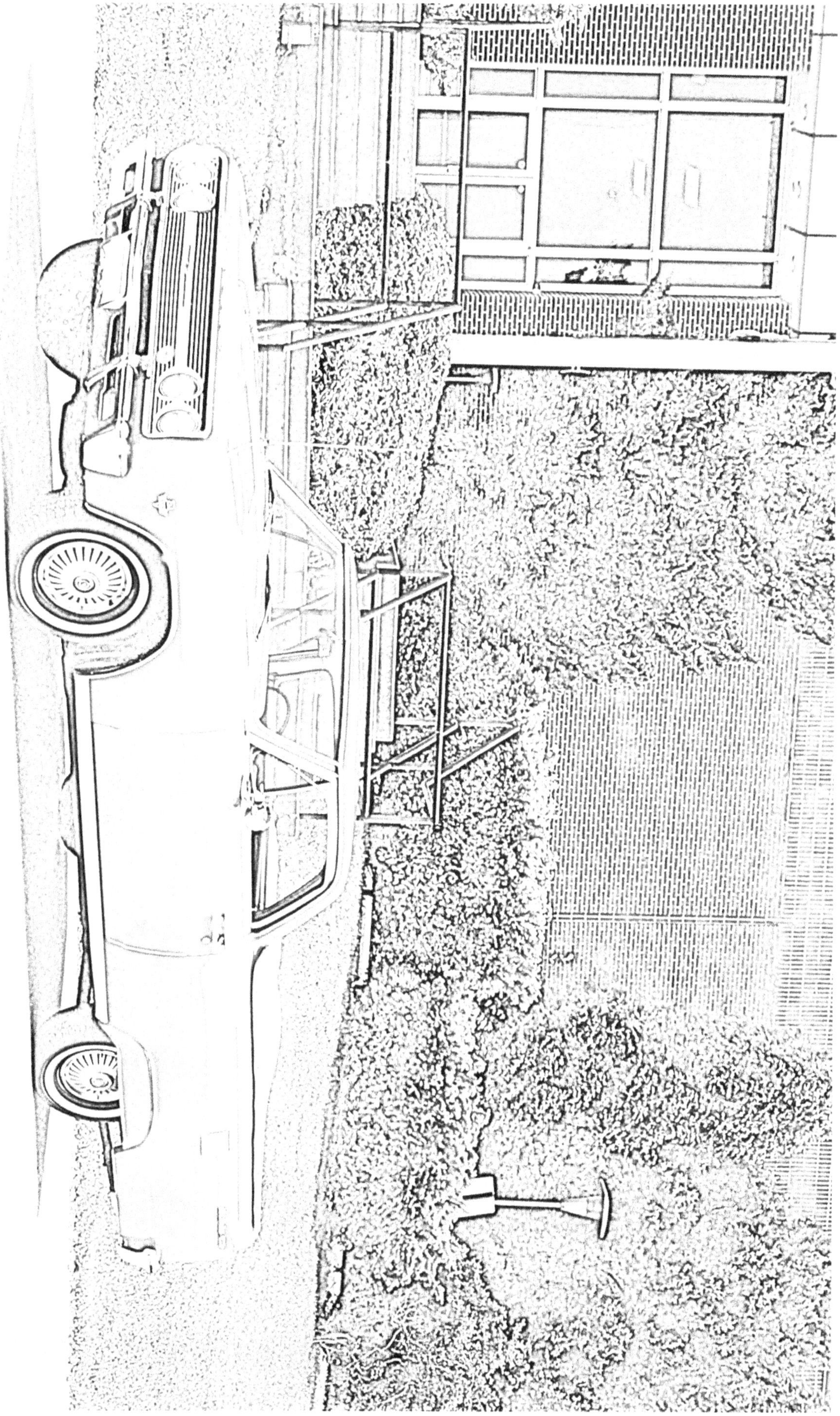

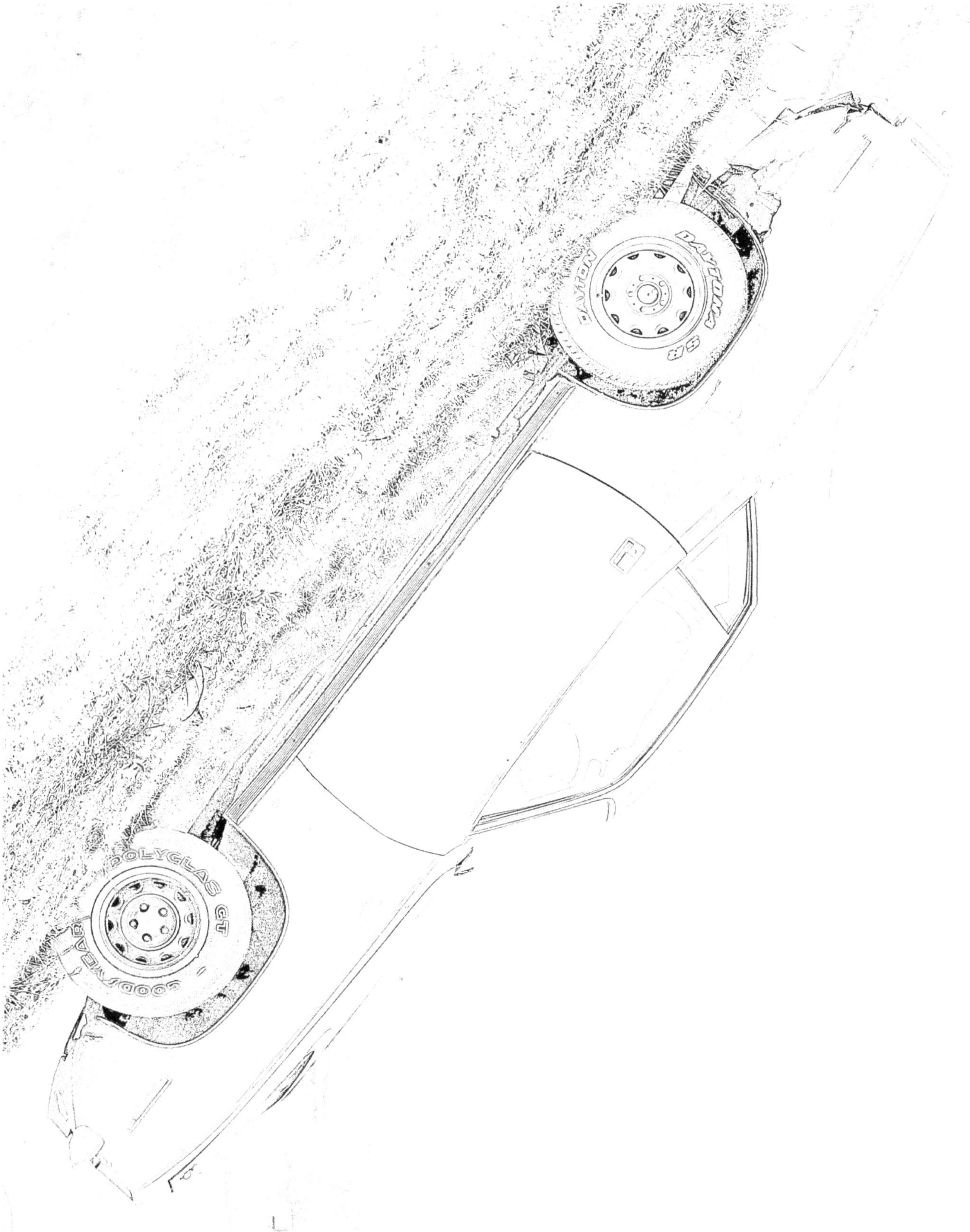
GOODYEAR
POLYGLAS GT
DAYTON
DAYTONA SR

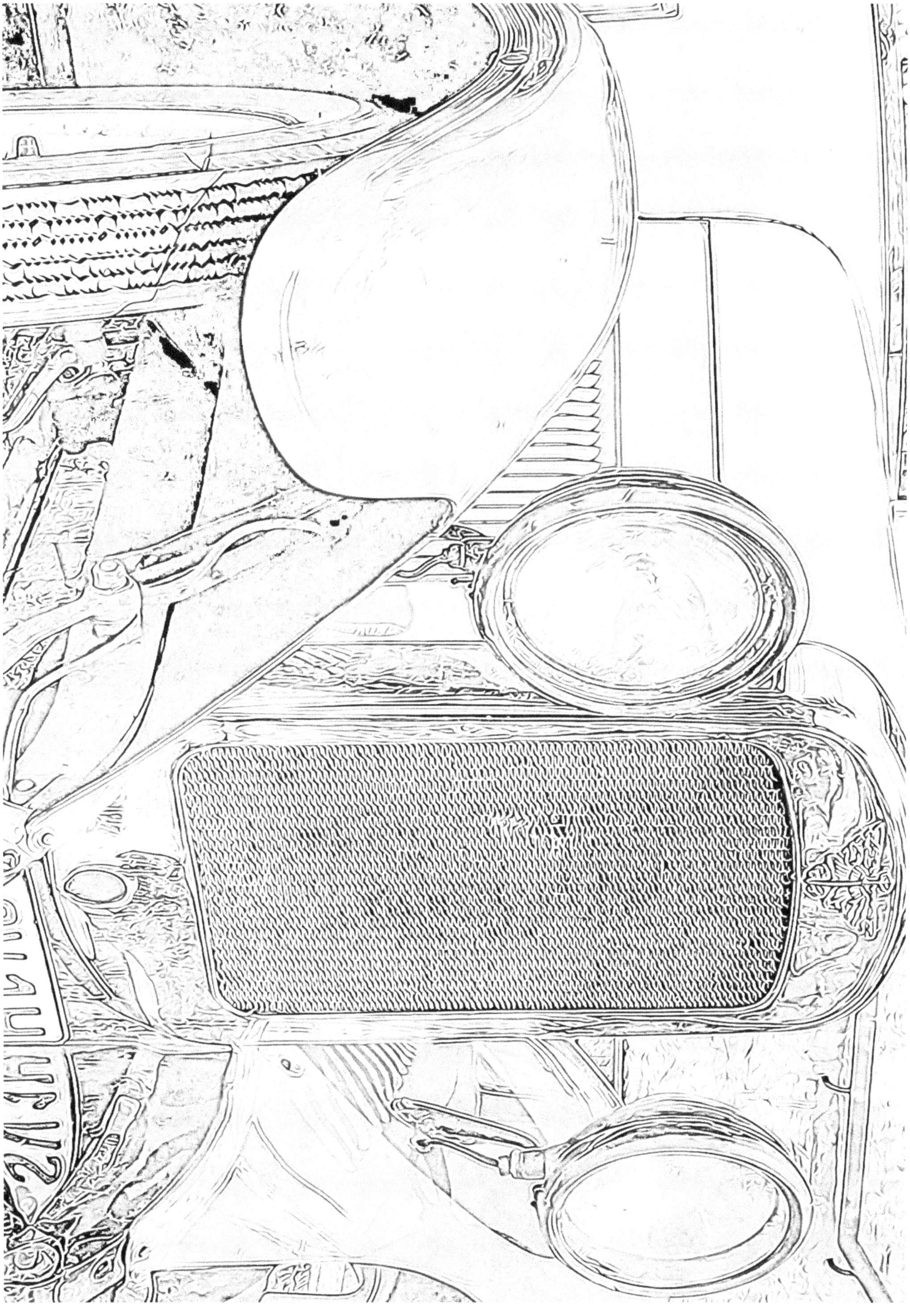

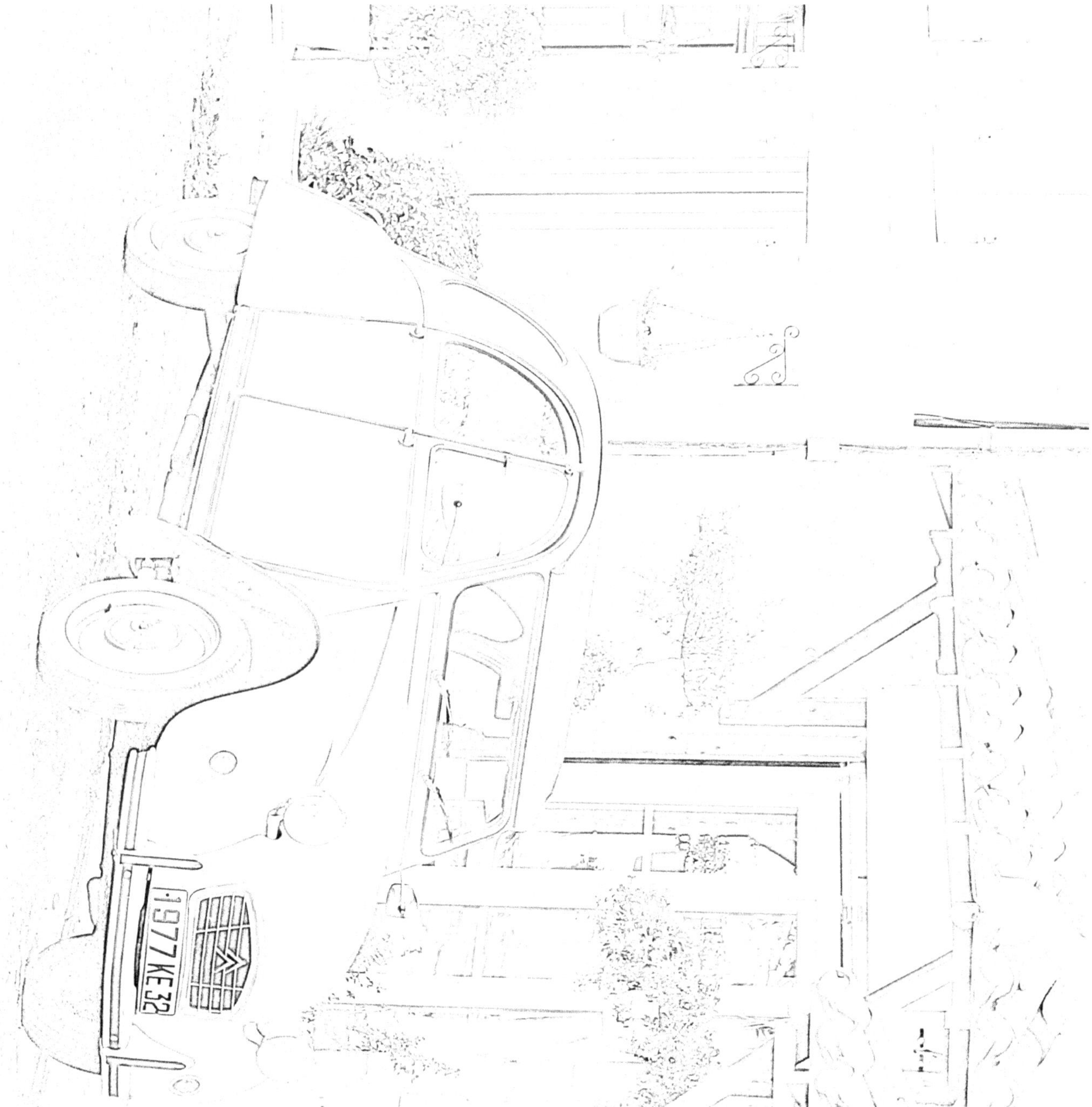
1977 KE 32

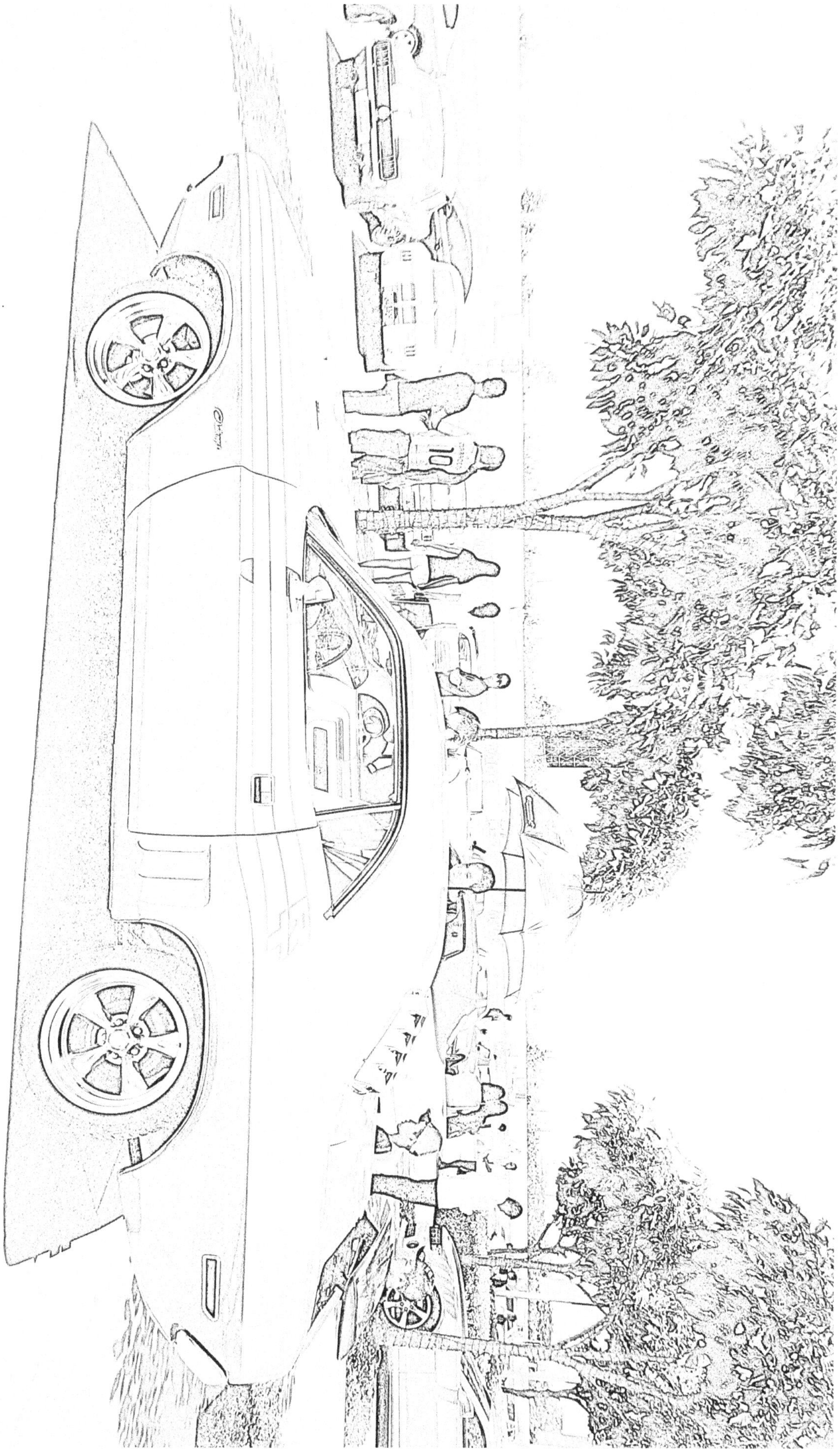

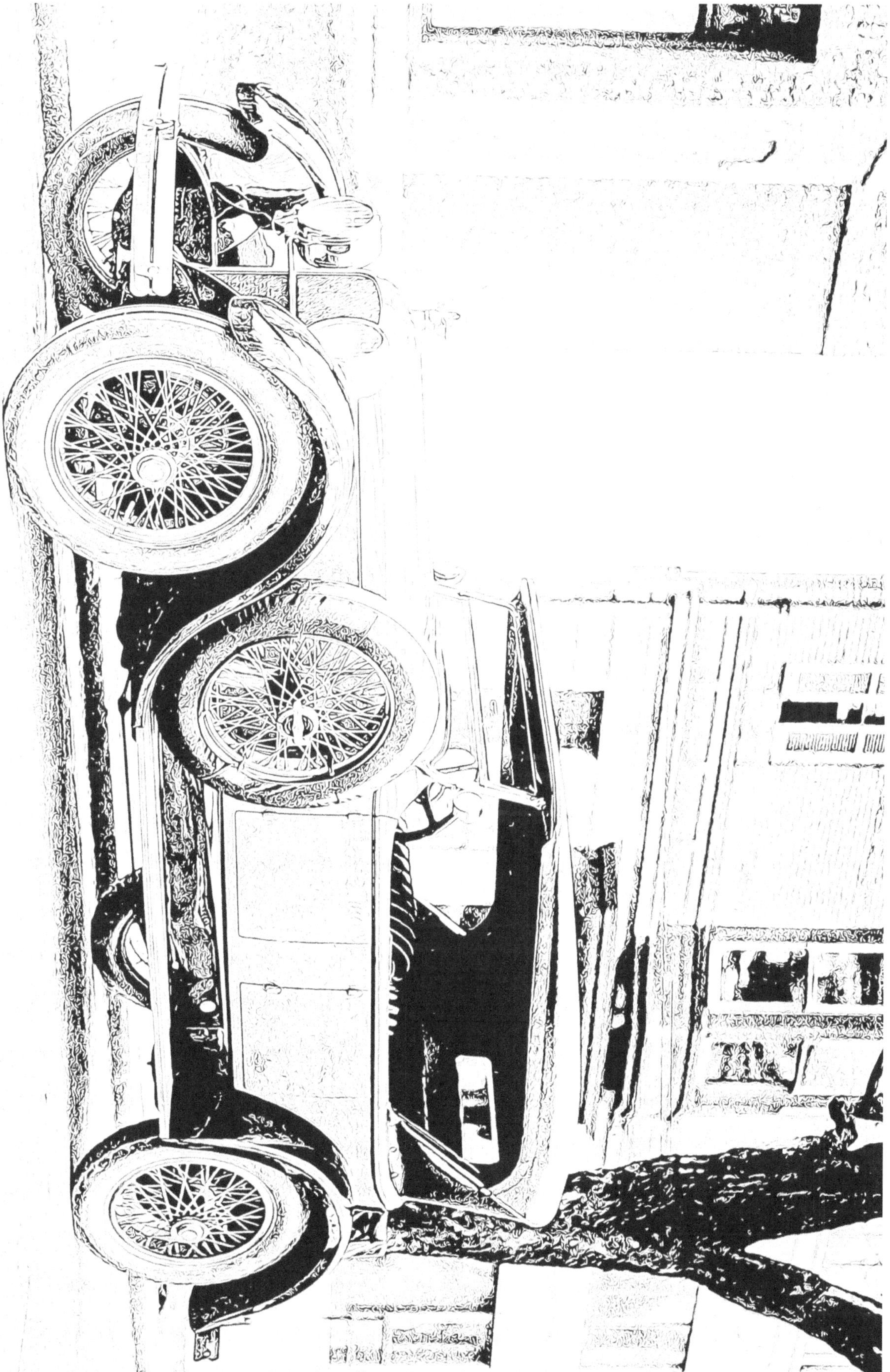

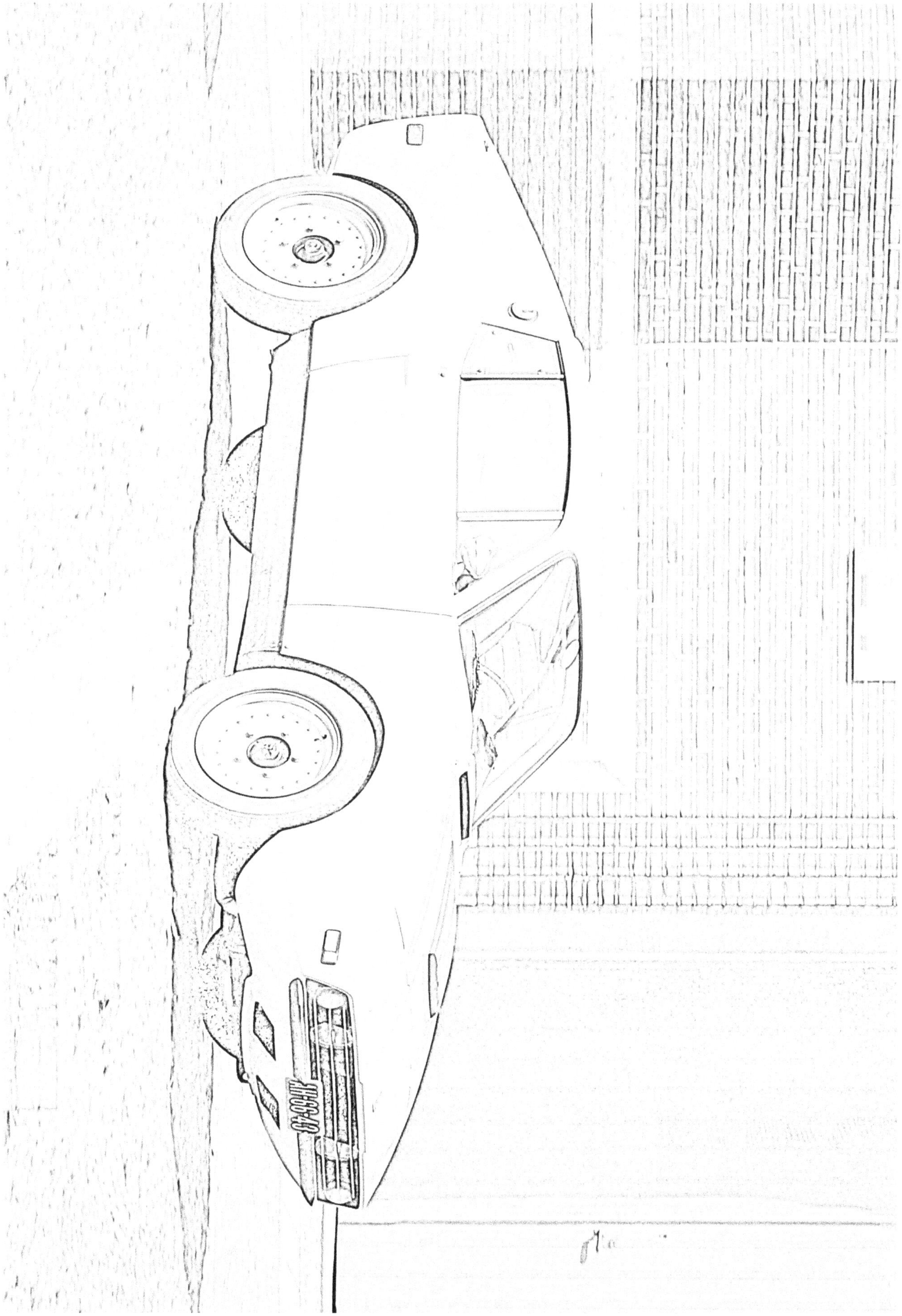

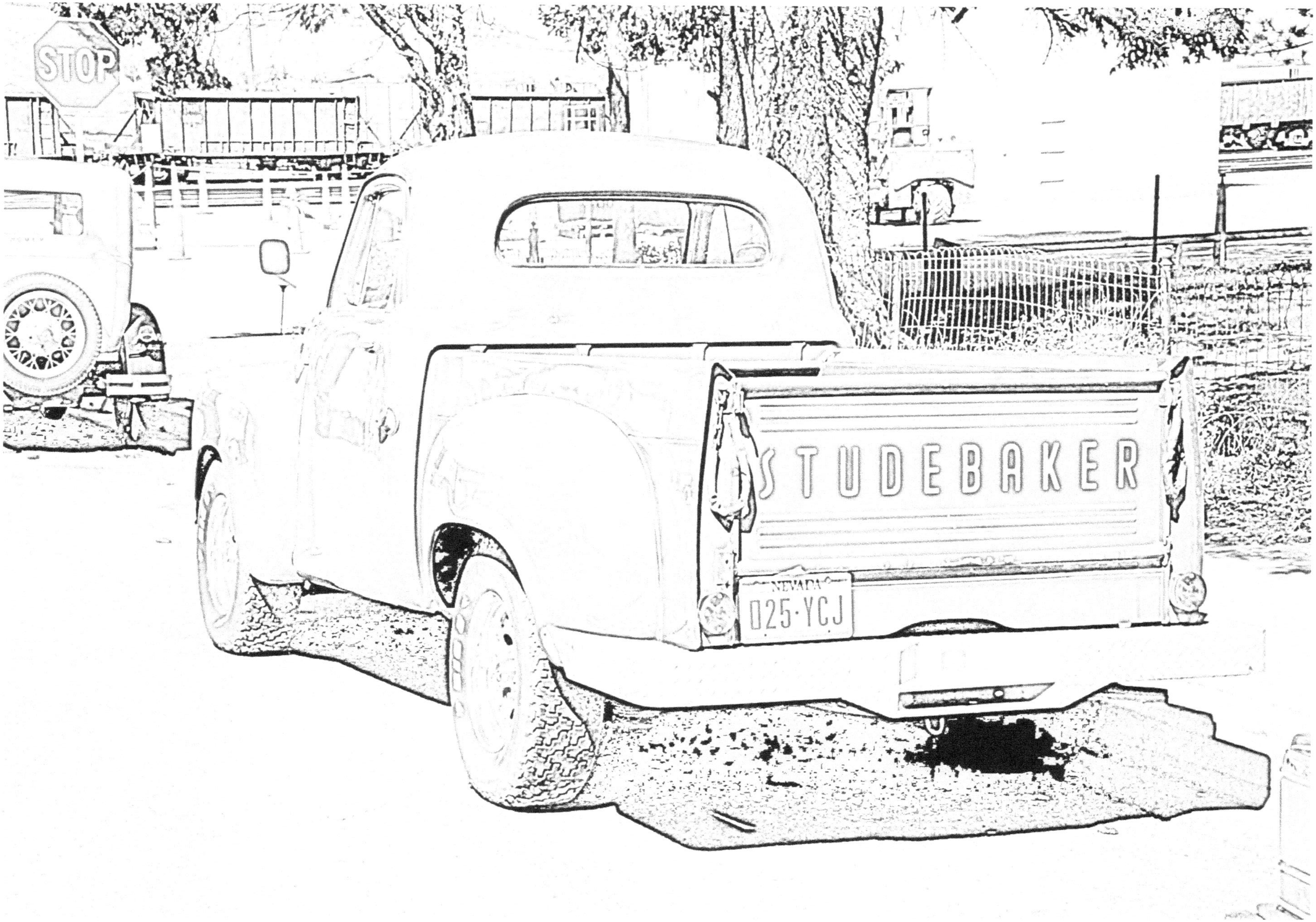
STOP
STUDEBAKER
NEVADA
D25·YCJ

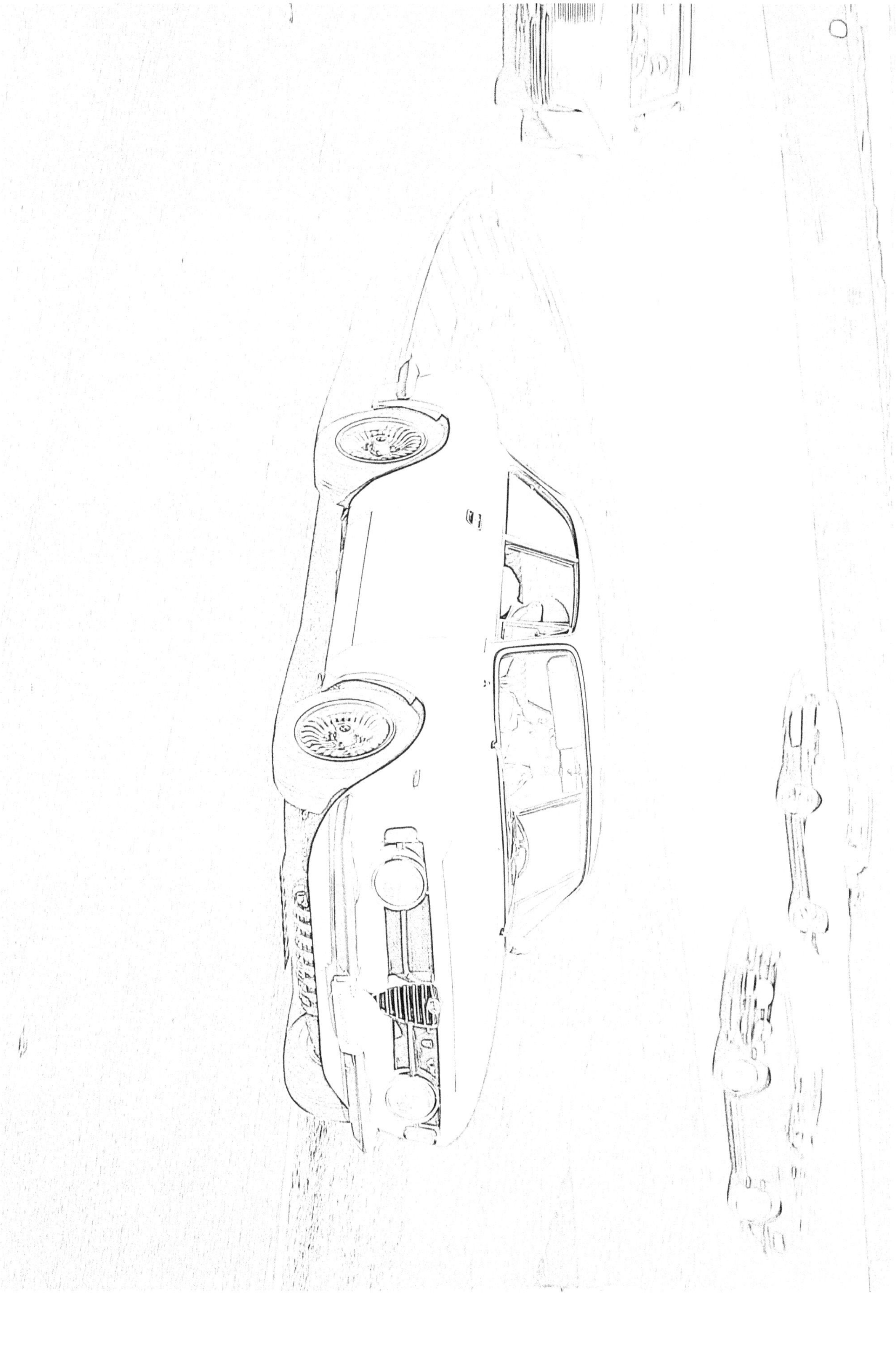

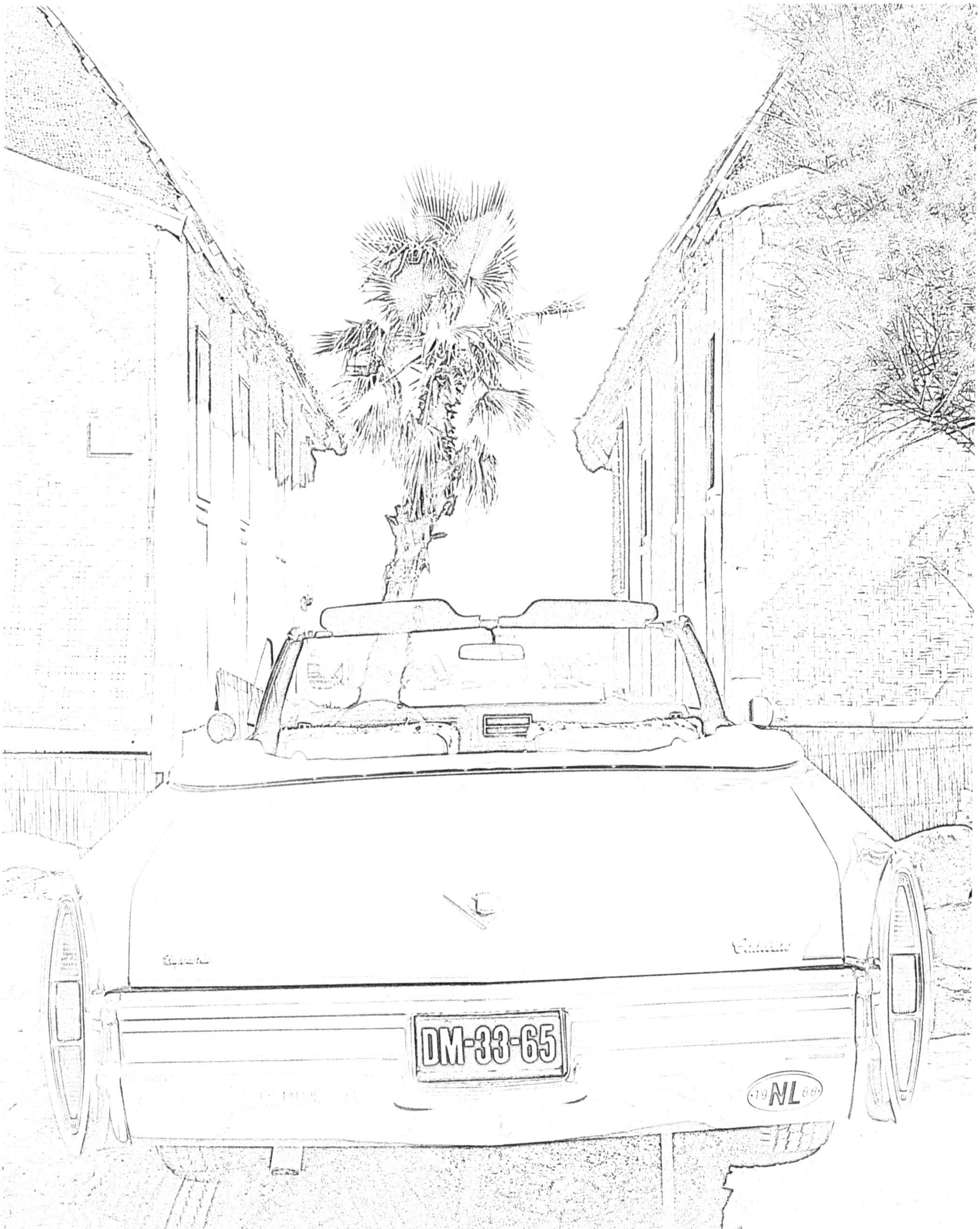
DM-33-65
NL

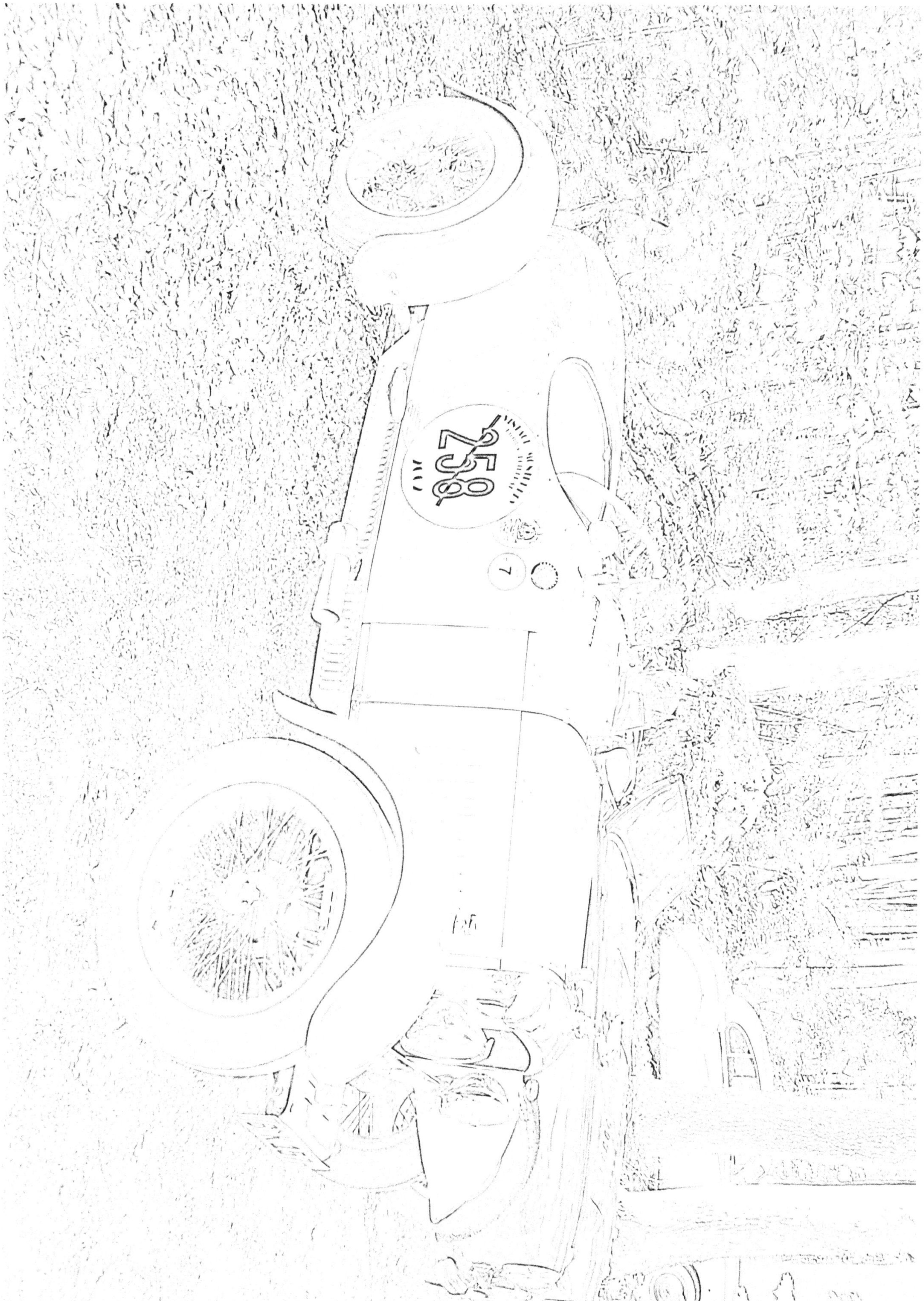
258

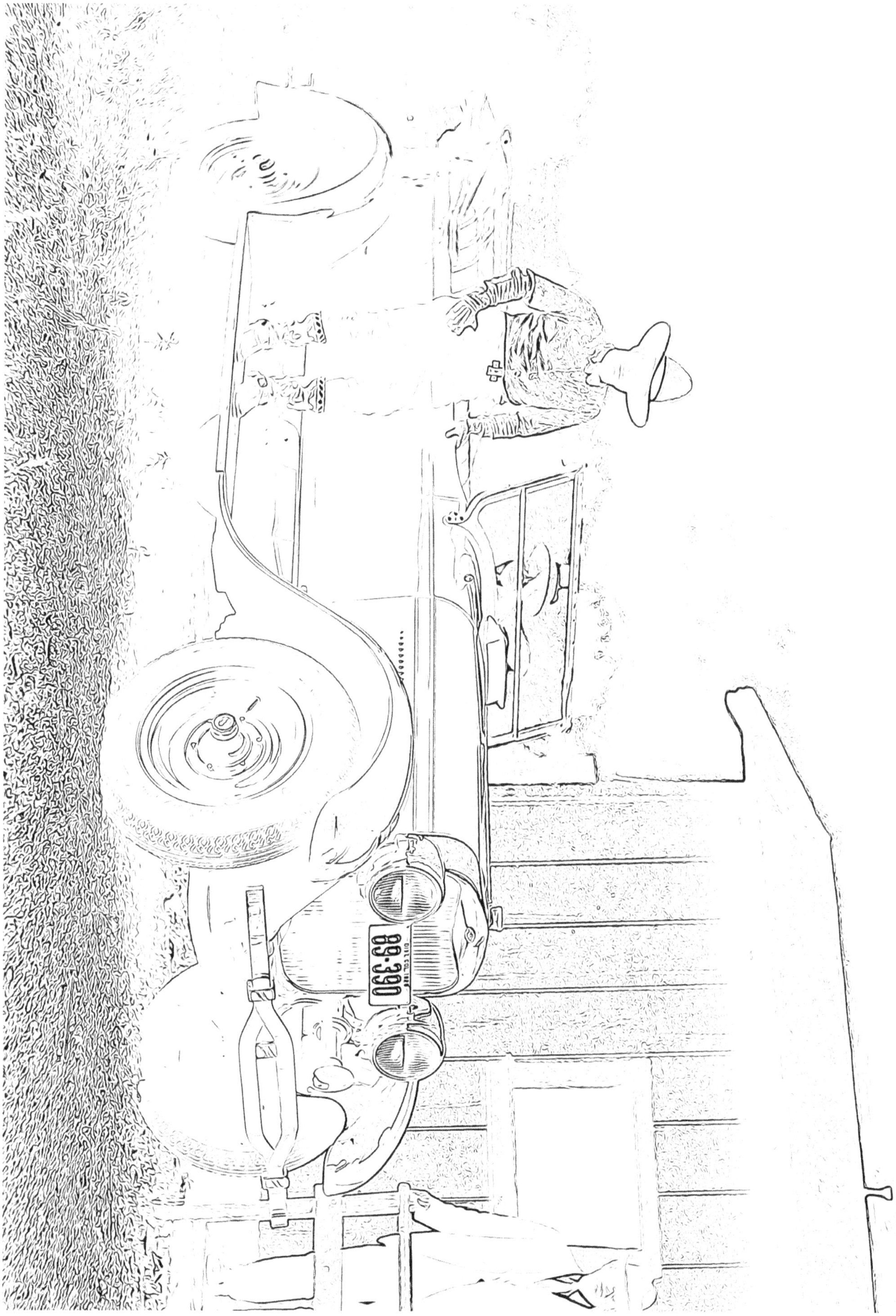
89-390

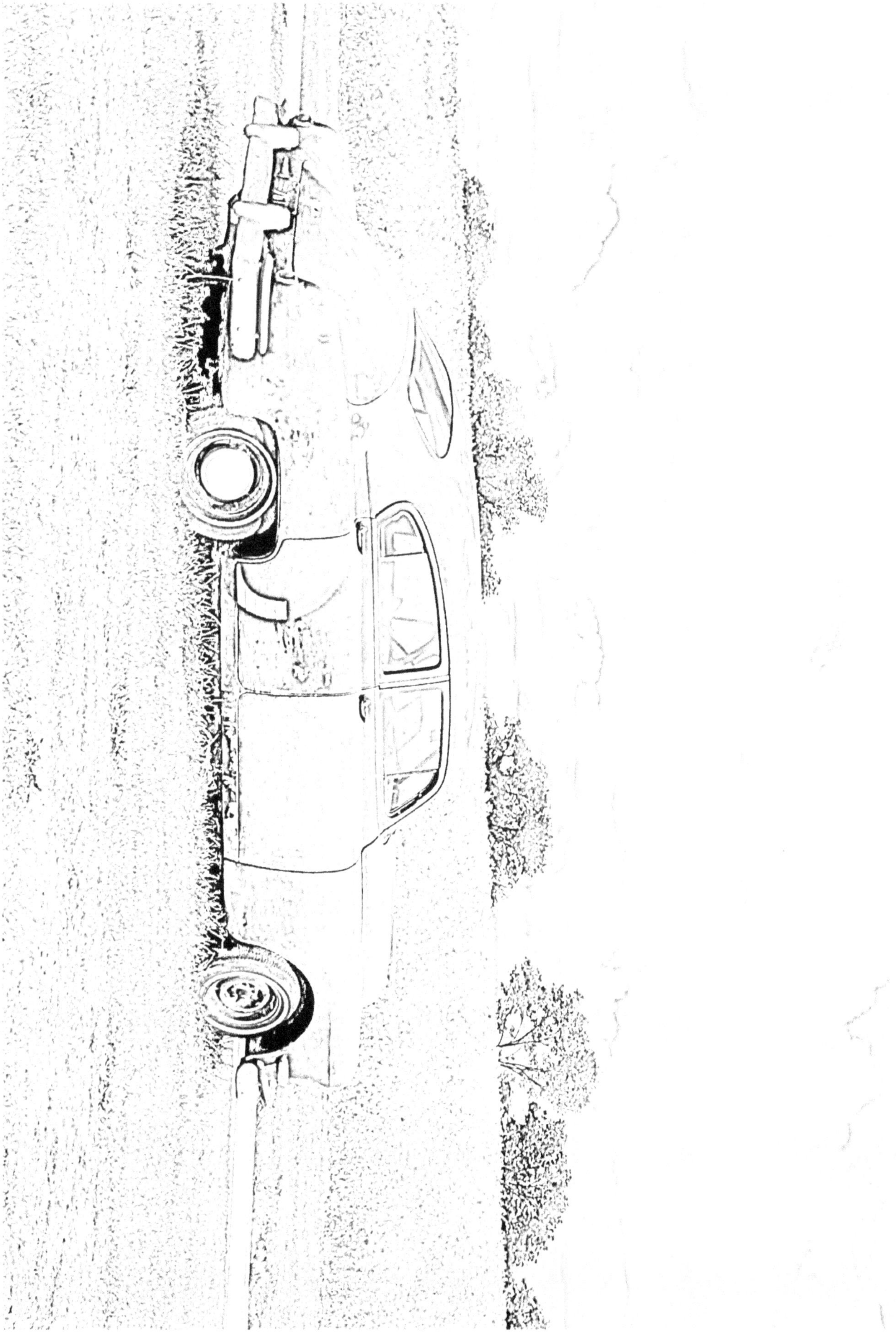

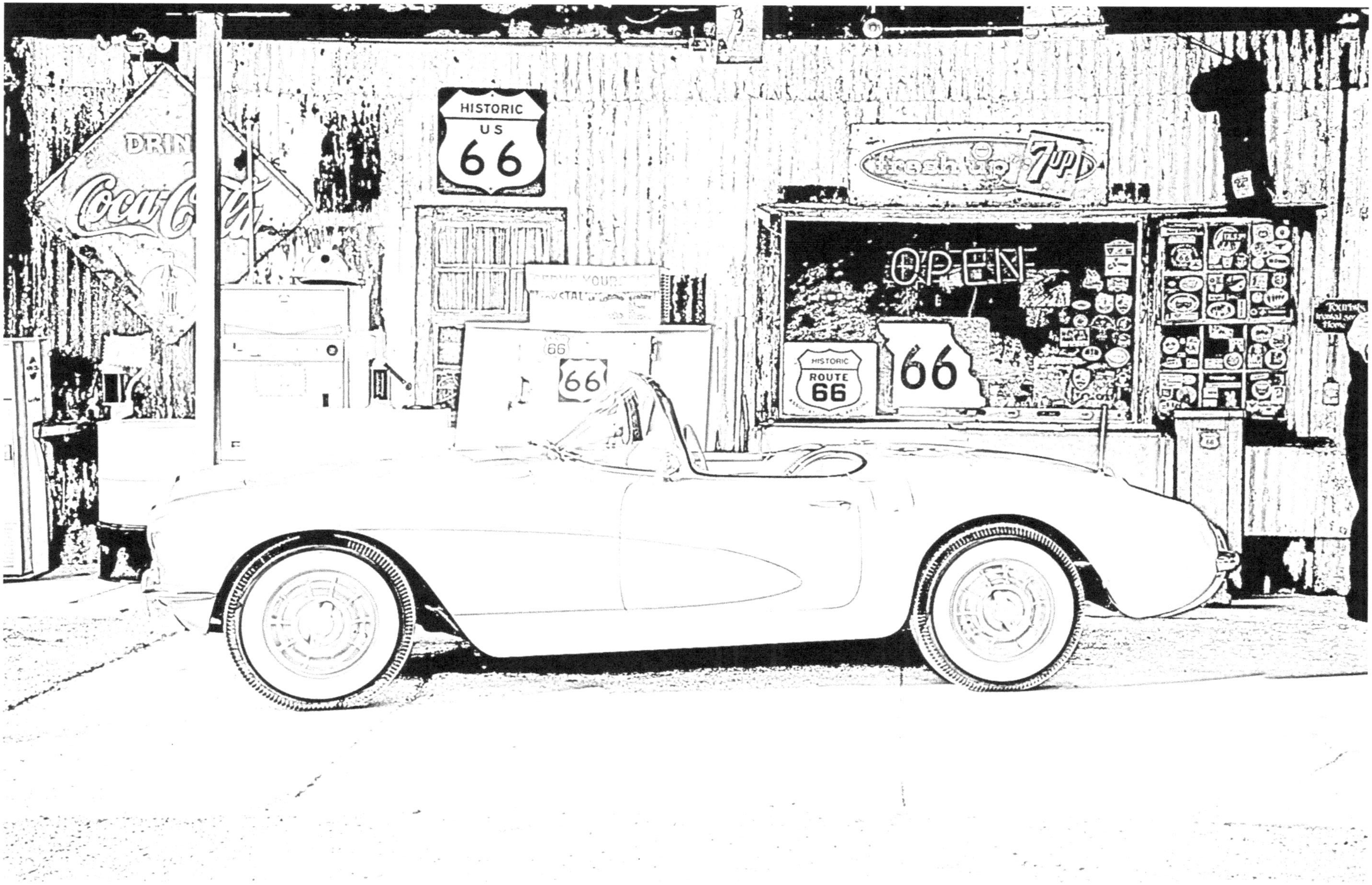
DRIN
Coca-Cola
HISTORIC
US
66
OPEN
66
HISTORIC
ROUTE
66
7UP

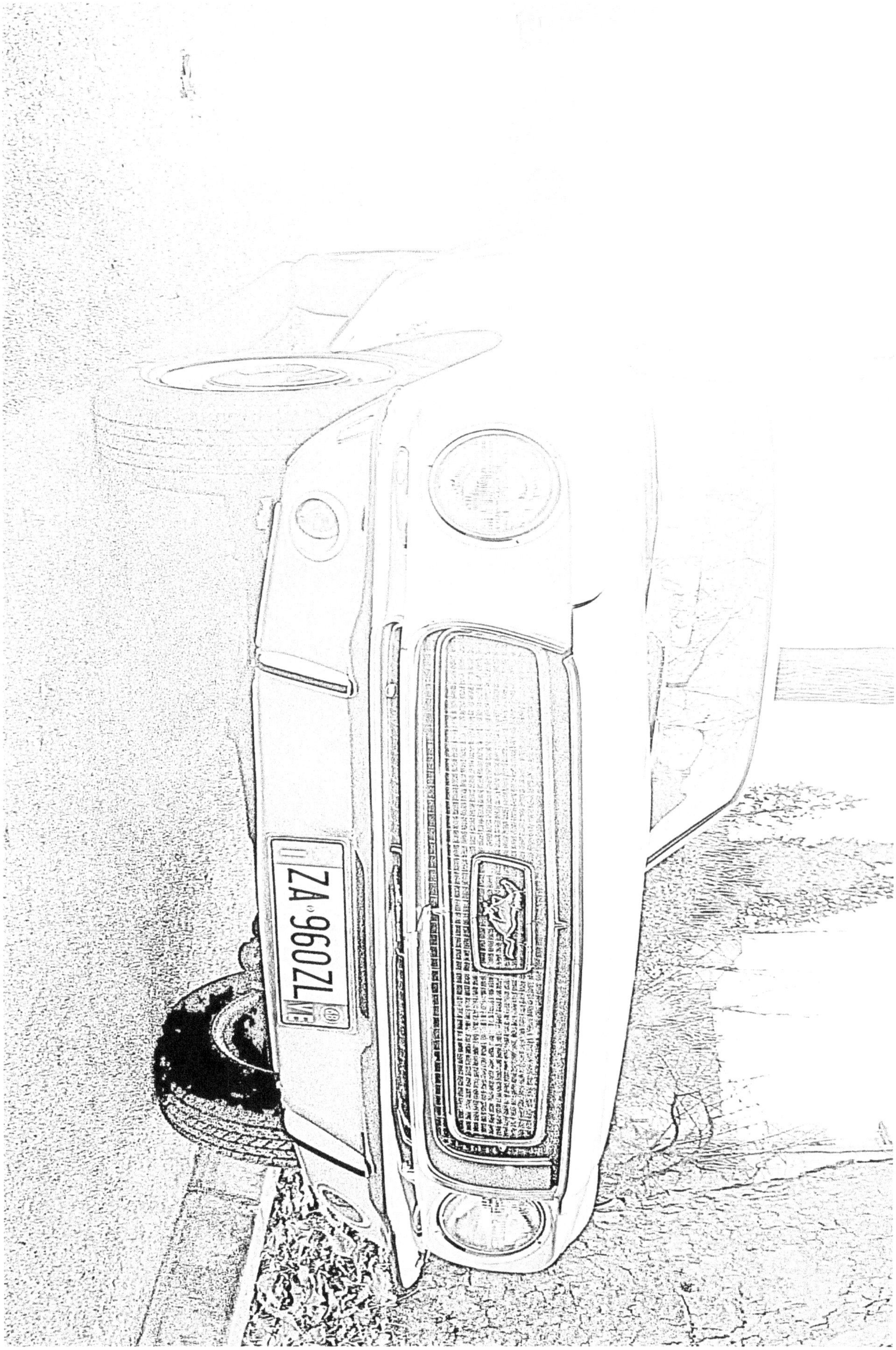
ZA 960ZL

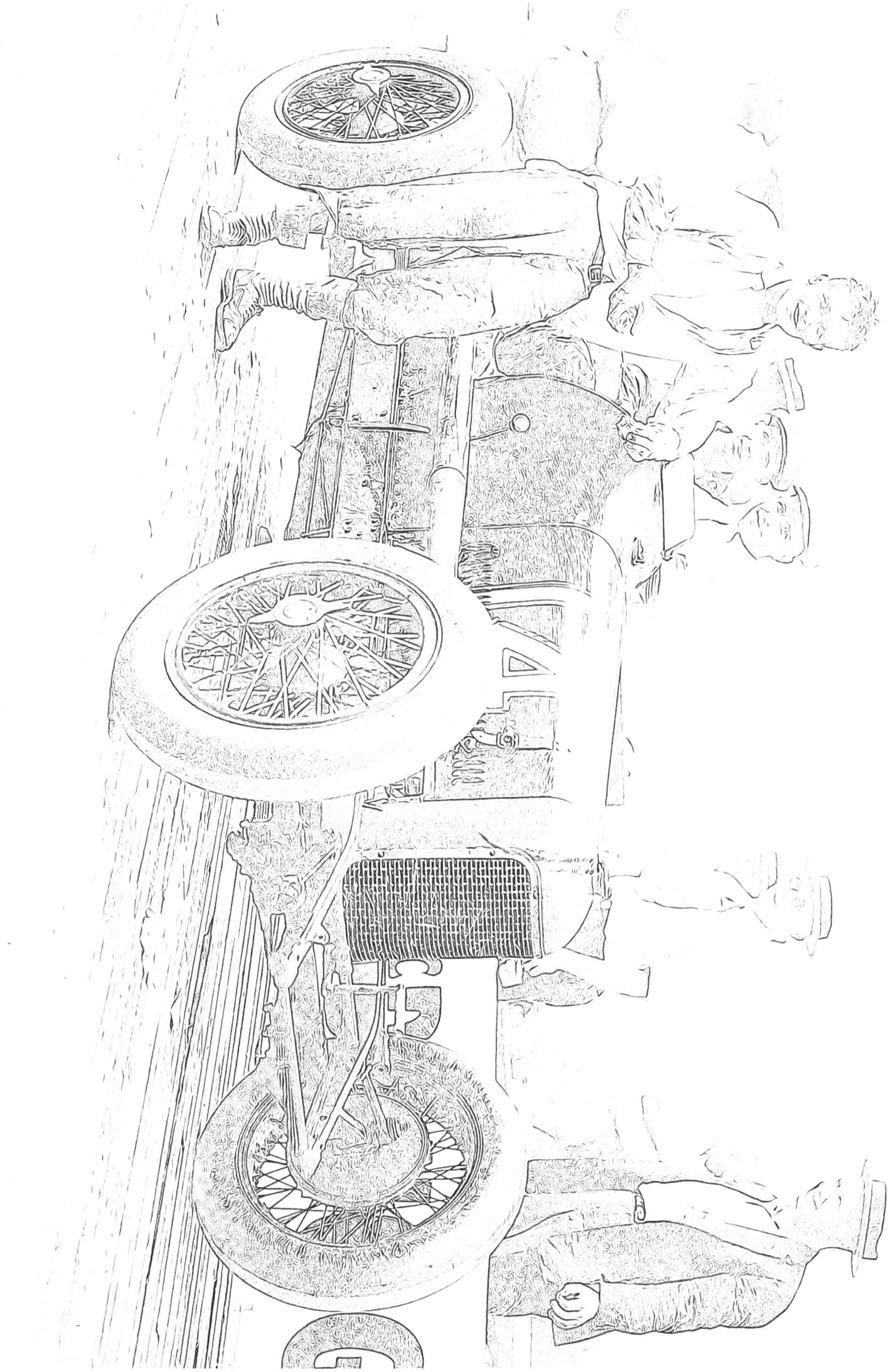

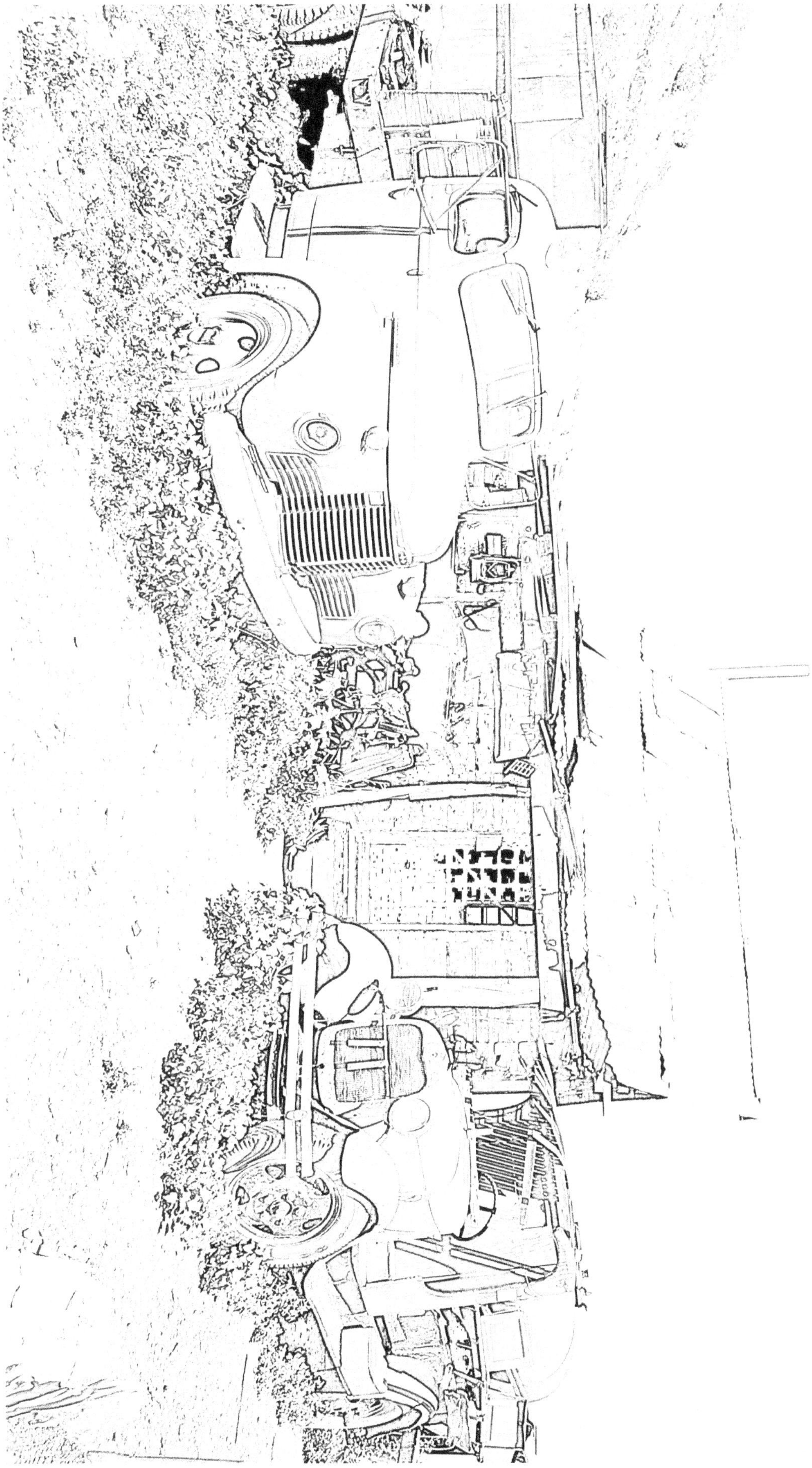

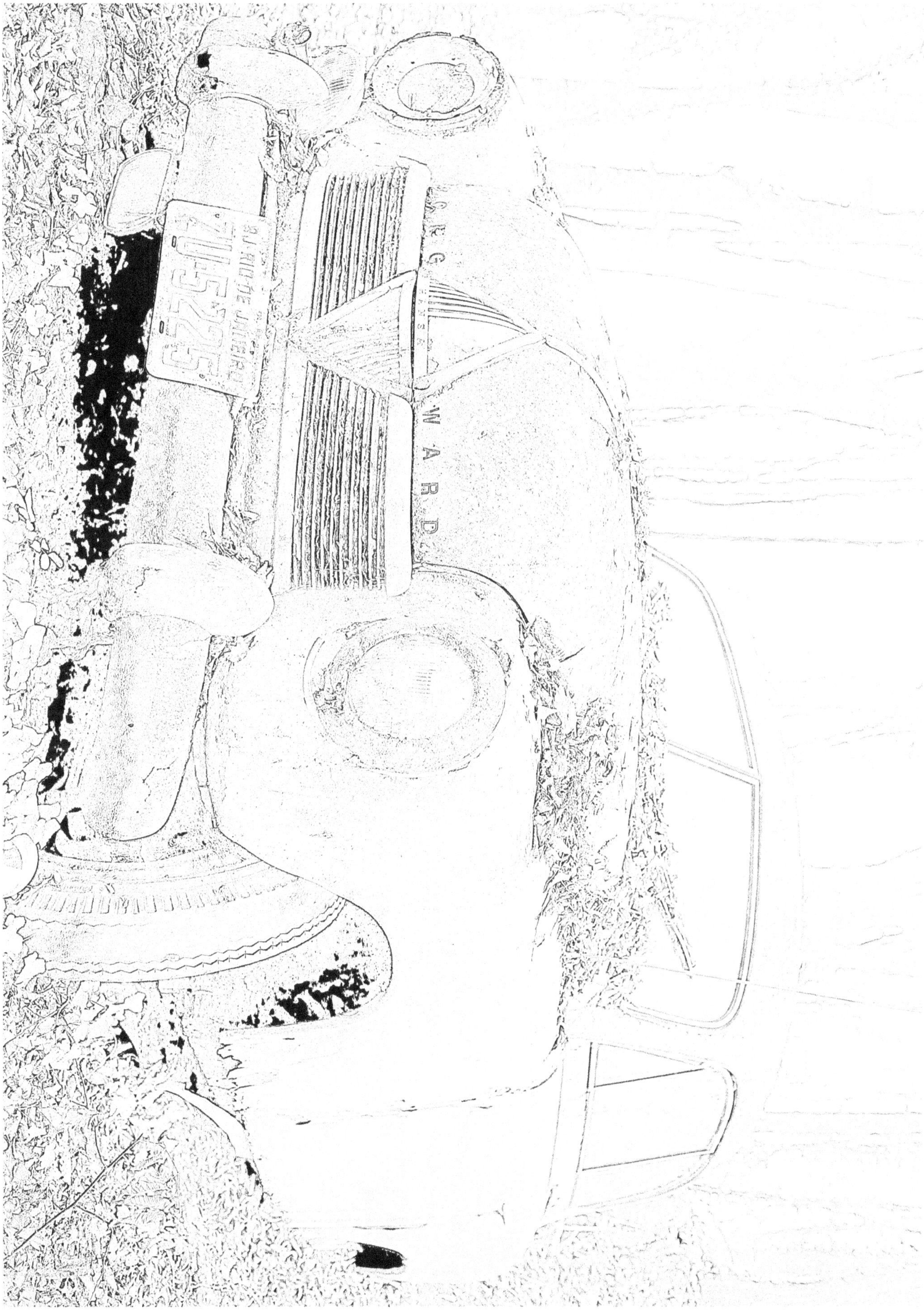

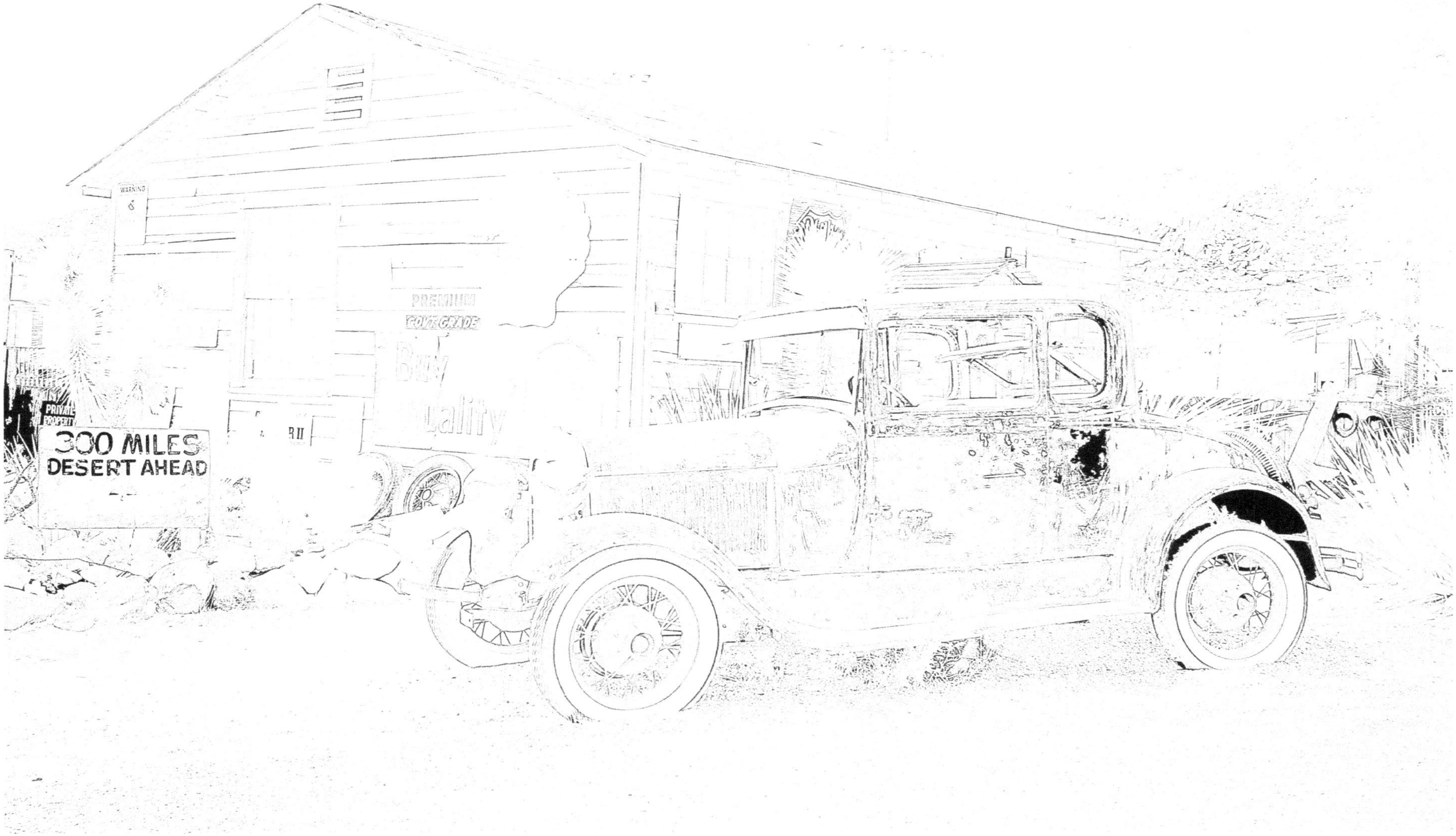
300 MILES
DESERT AHEAD
PREMIUM
GOV'T GRADE

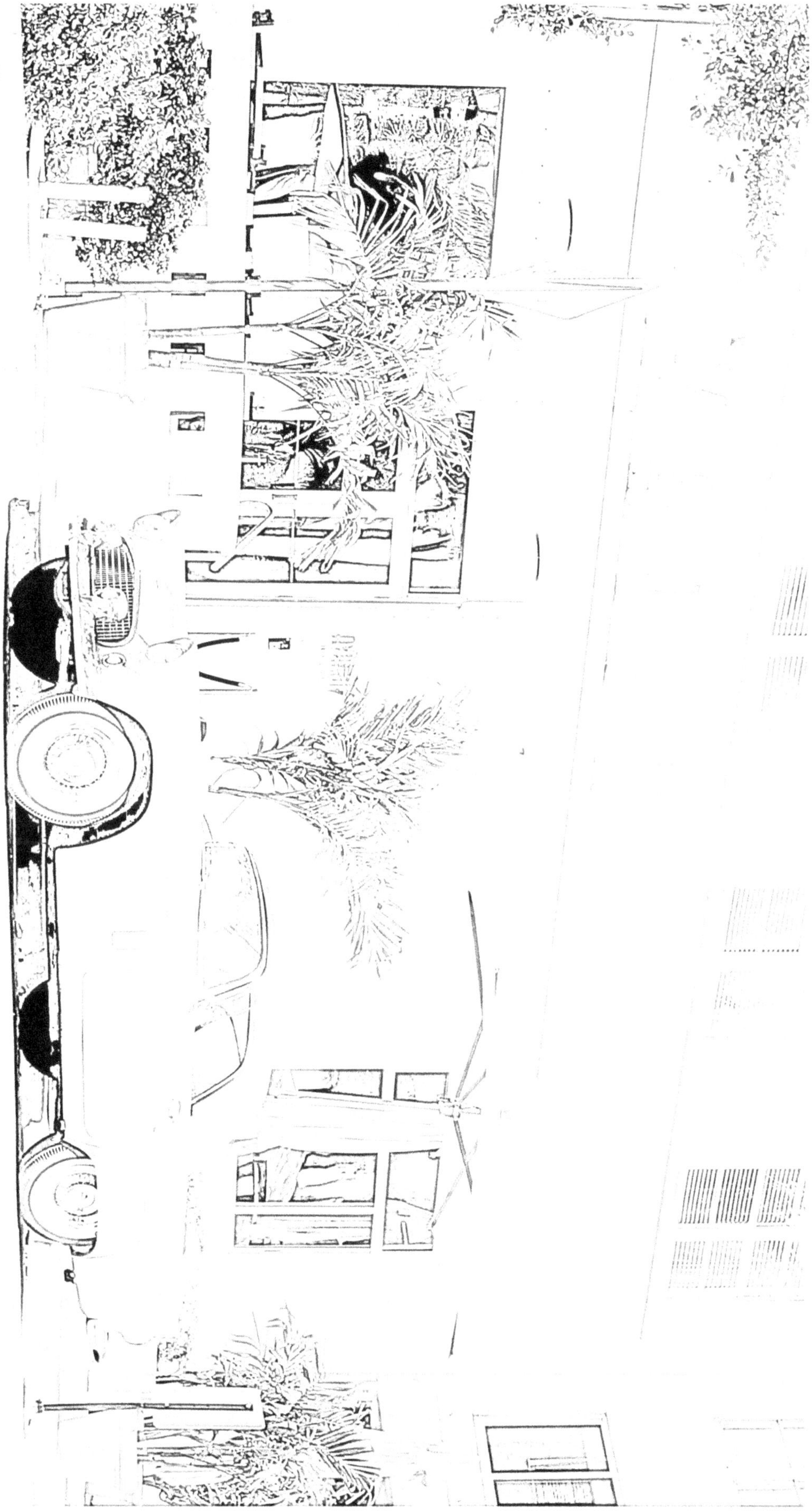

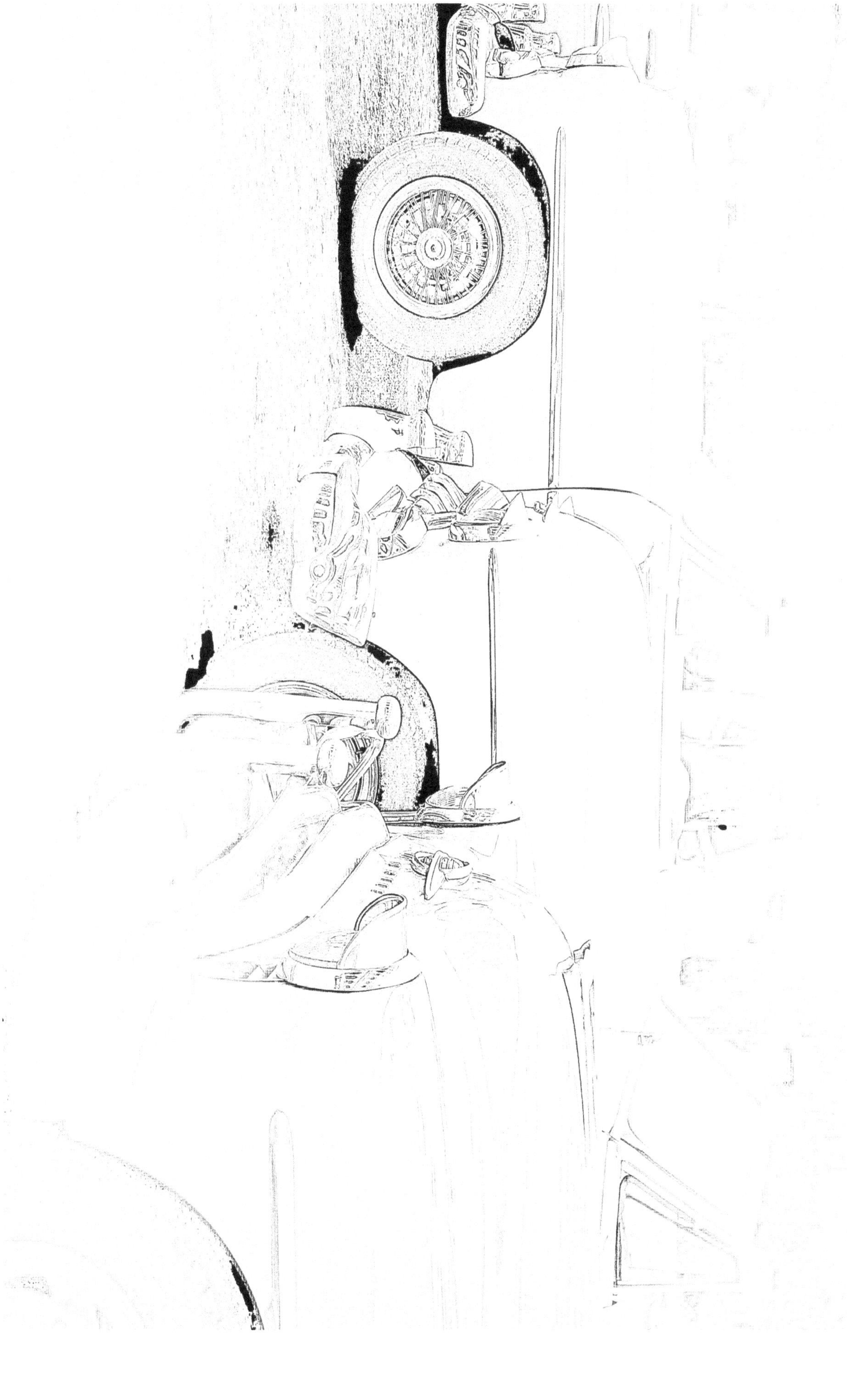

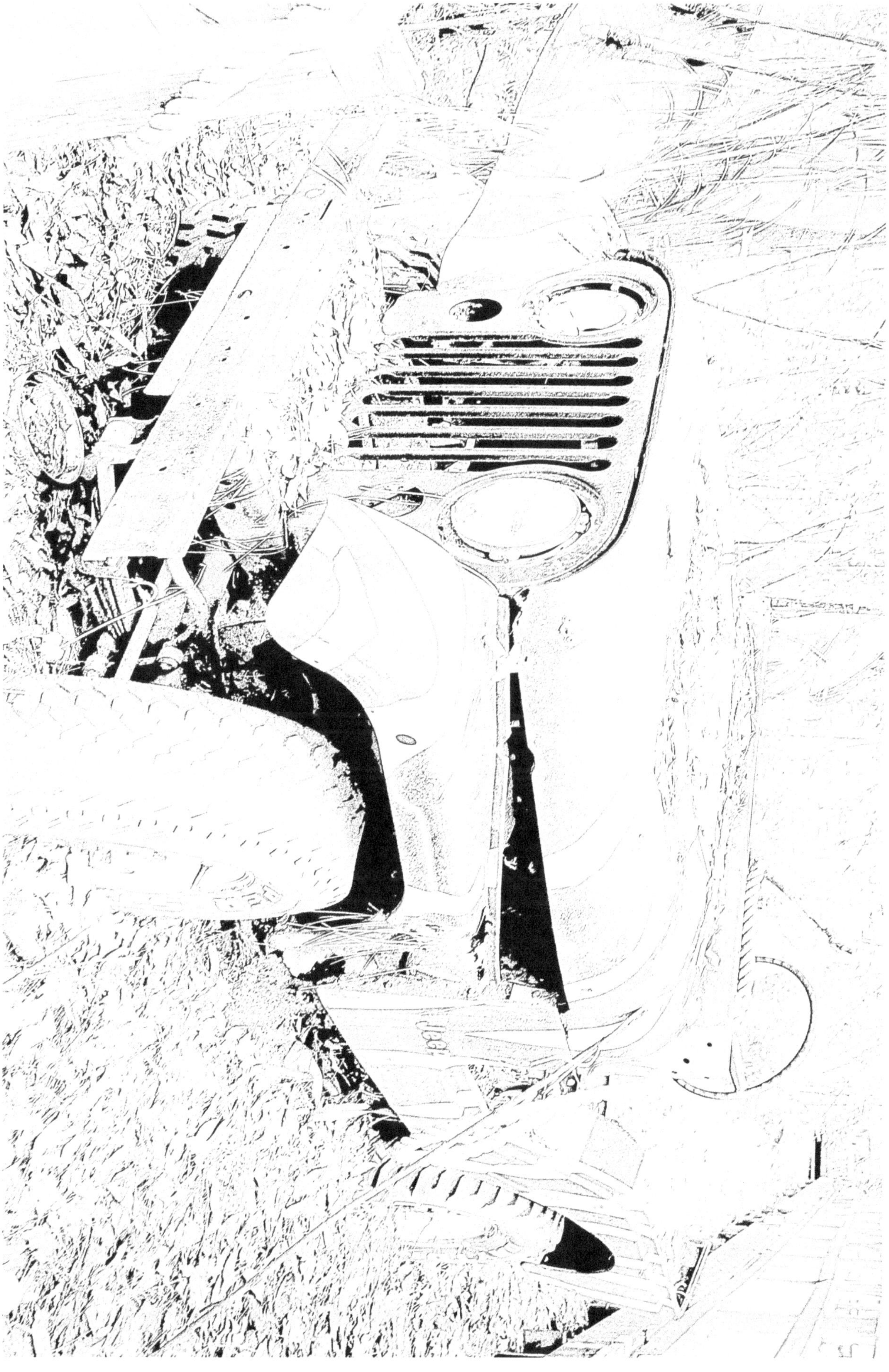

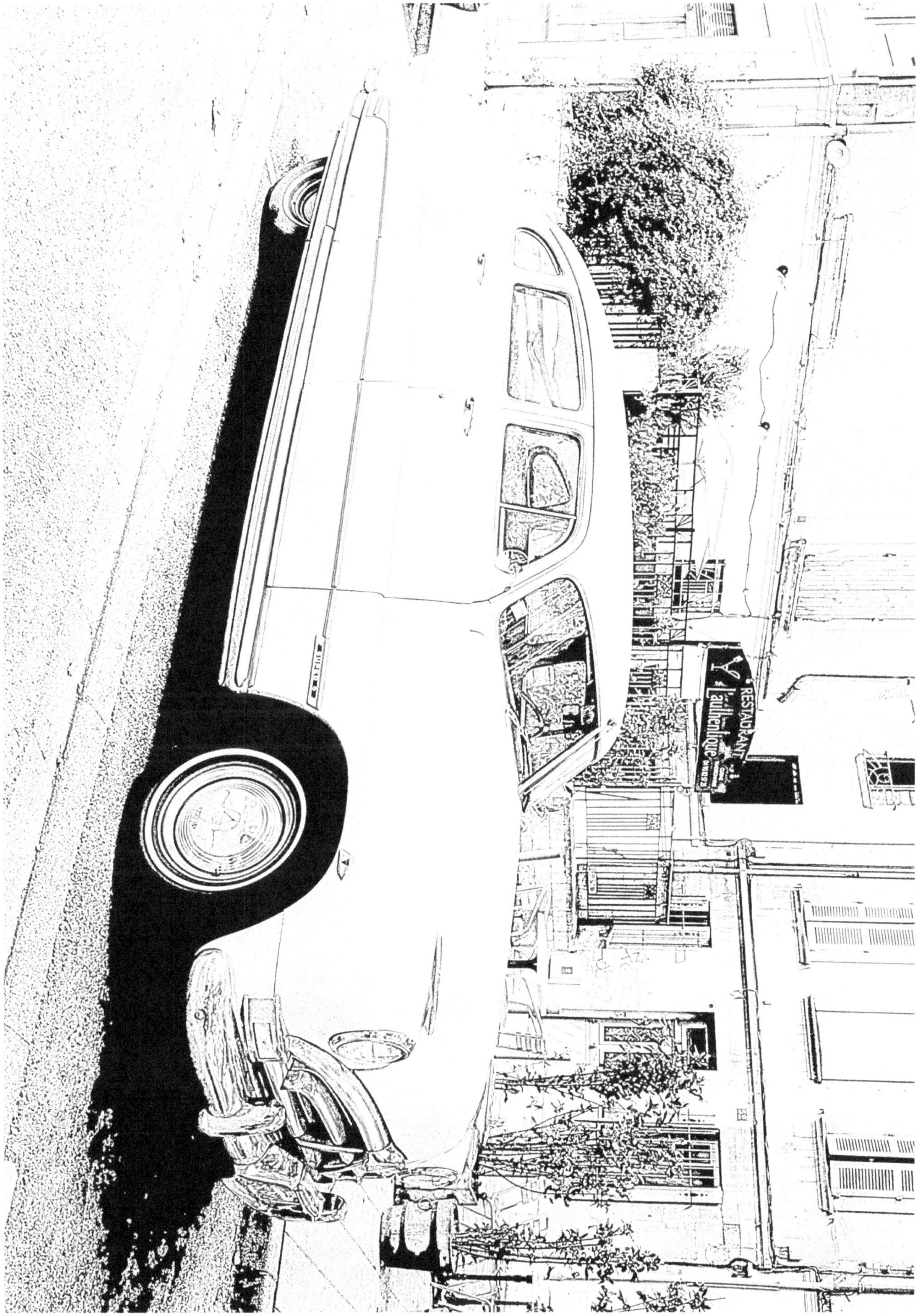
RESTAURANT
L'authentique

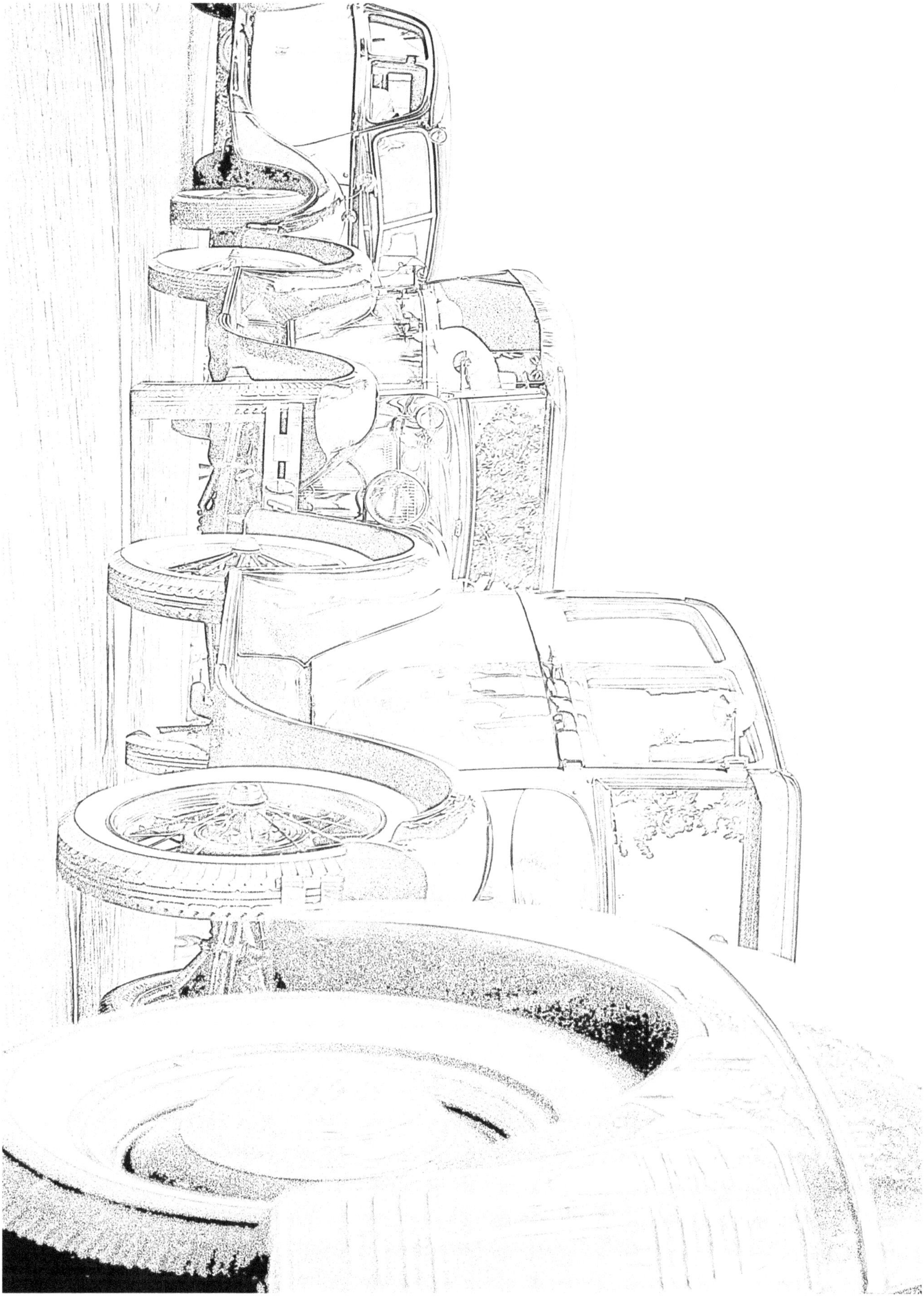

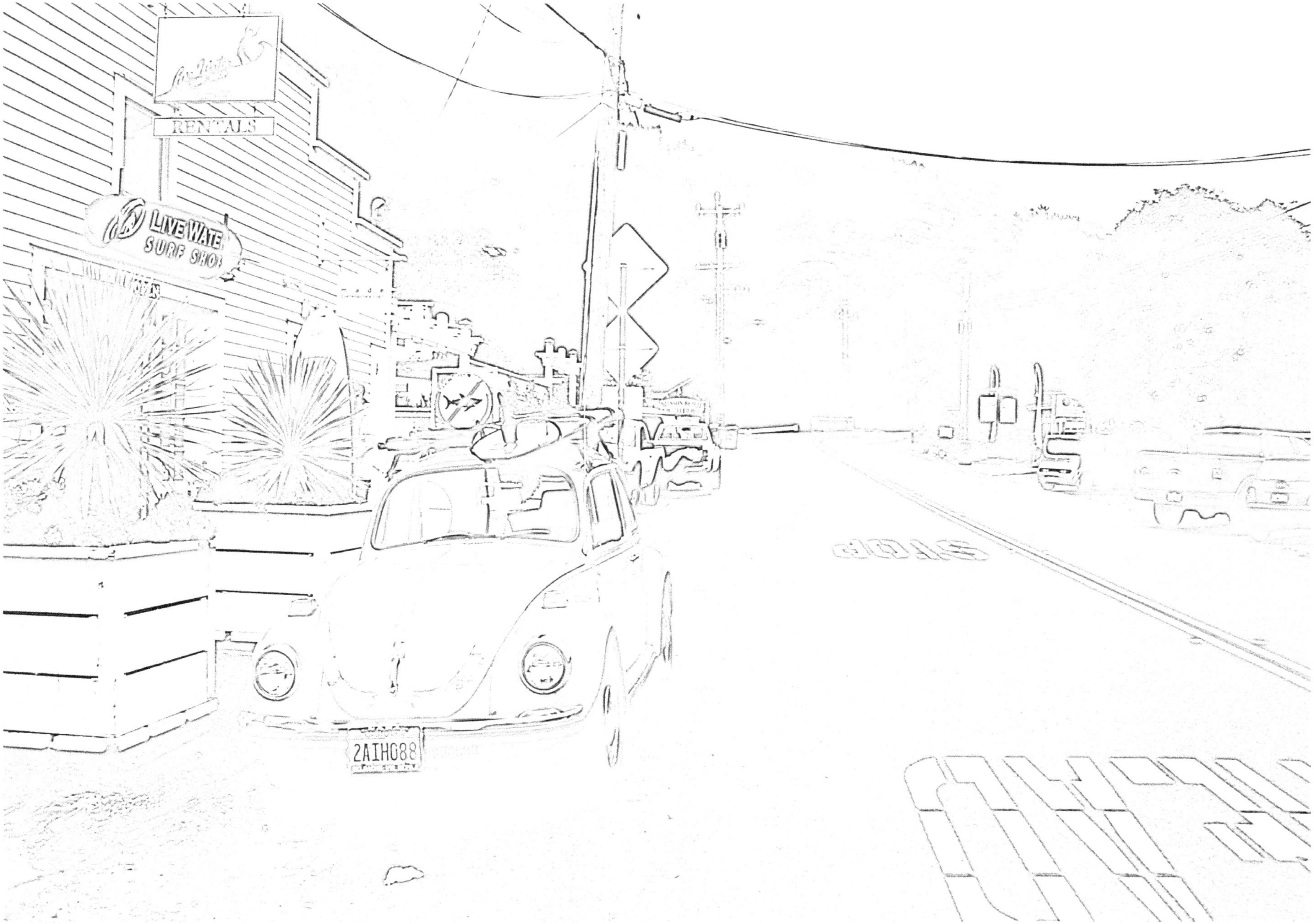
RENTALS
LIVE WATE
SURF SHO
2AIH088

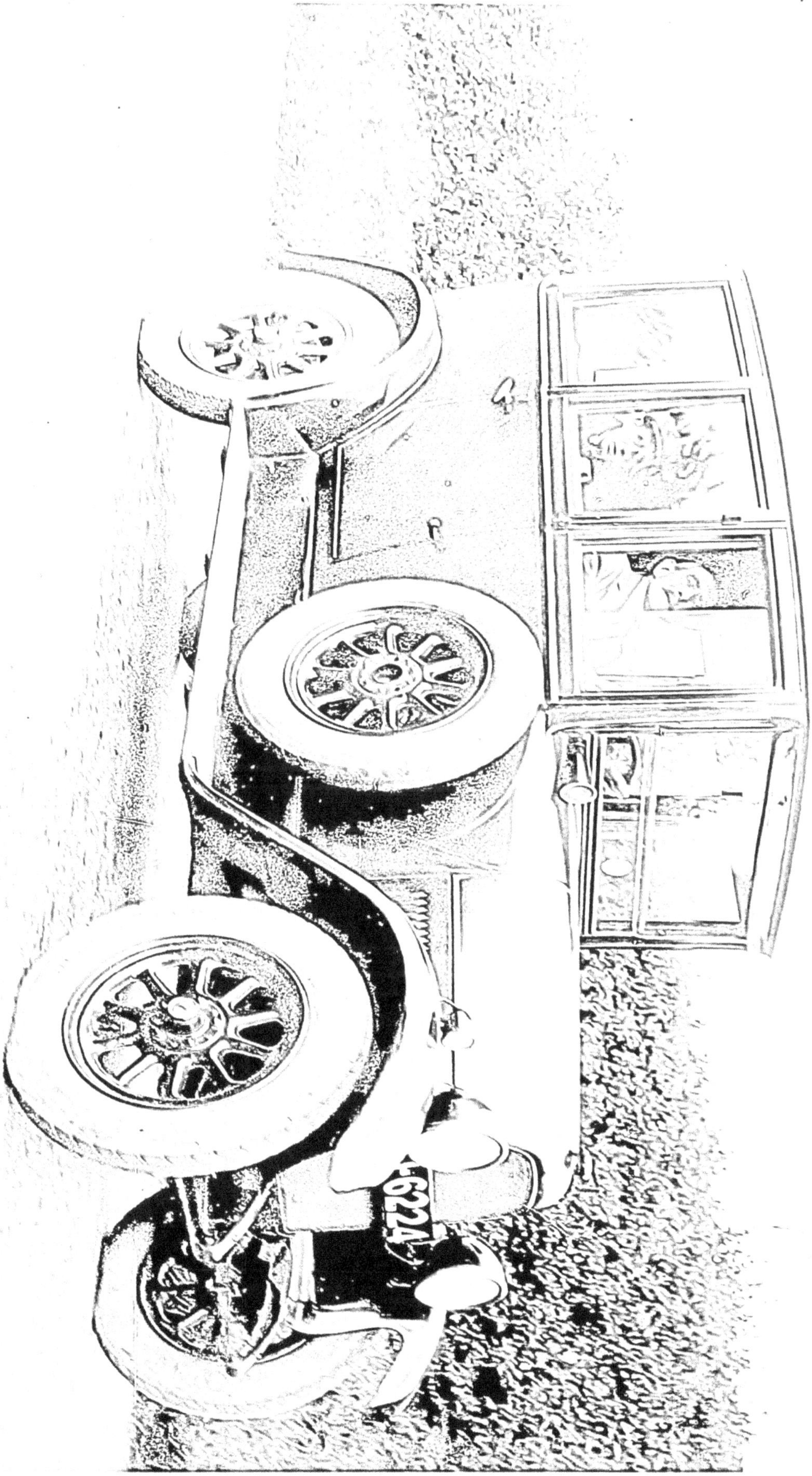
6224

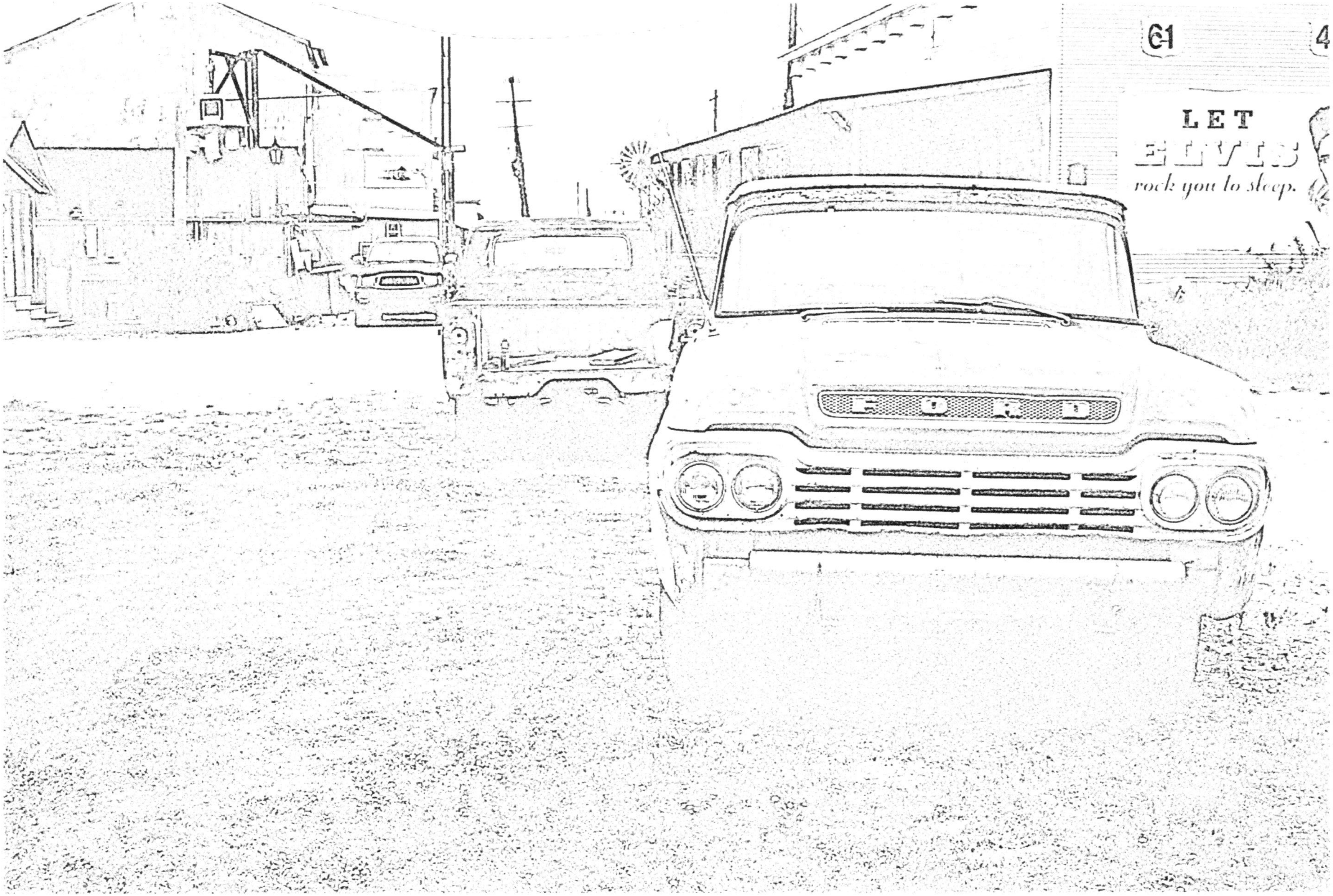
61
LET
ELVIS
rock you to sleep.
FORD

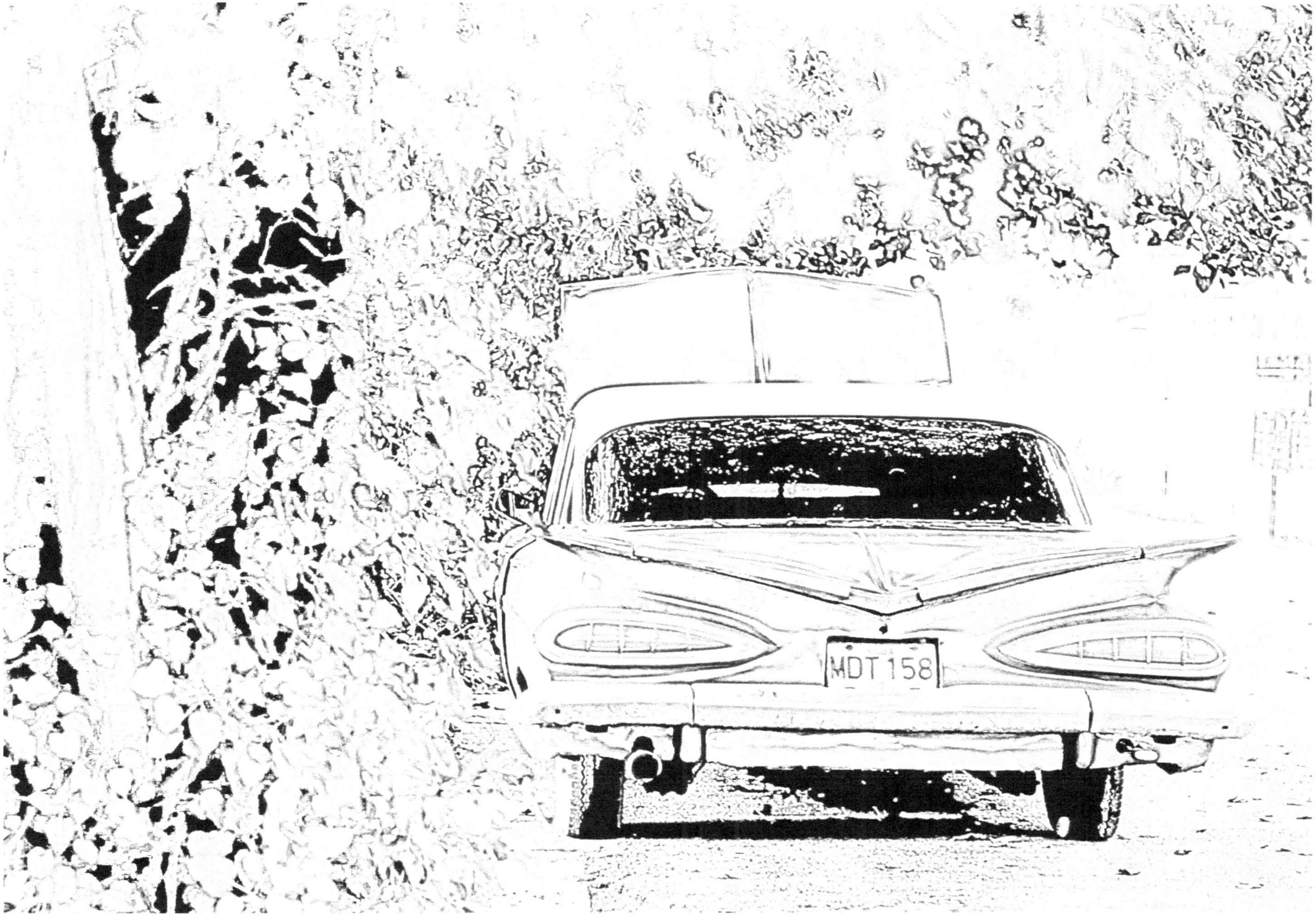
MDT 158

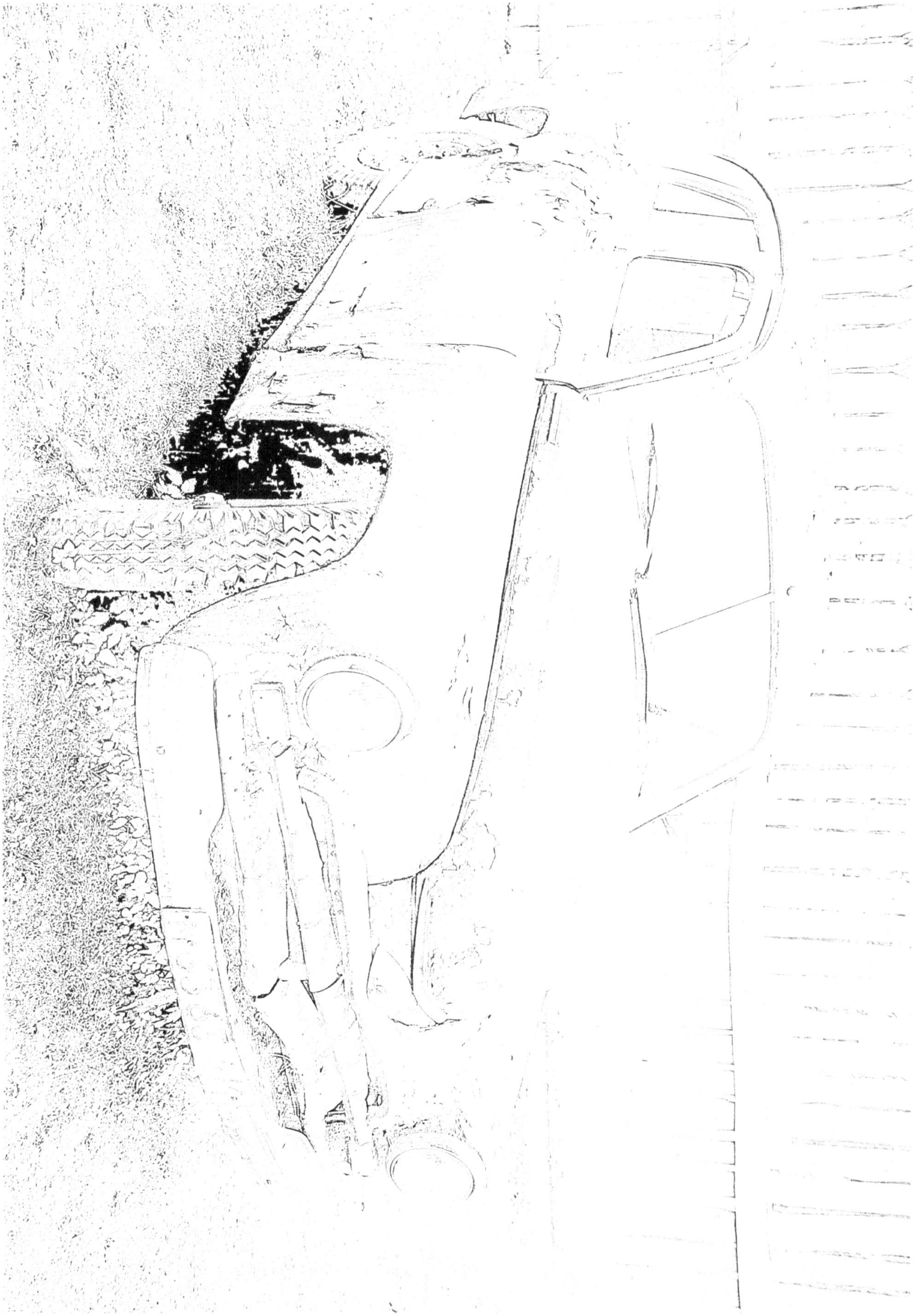

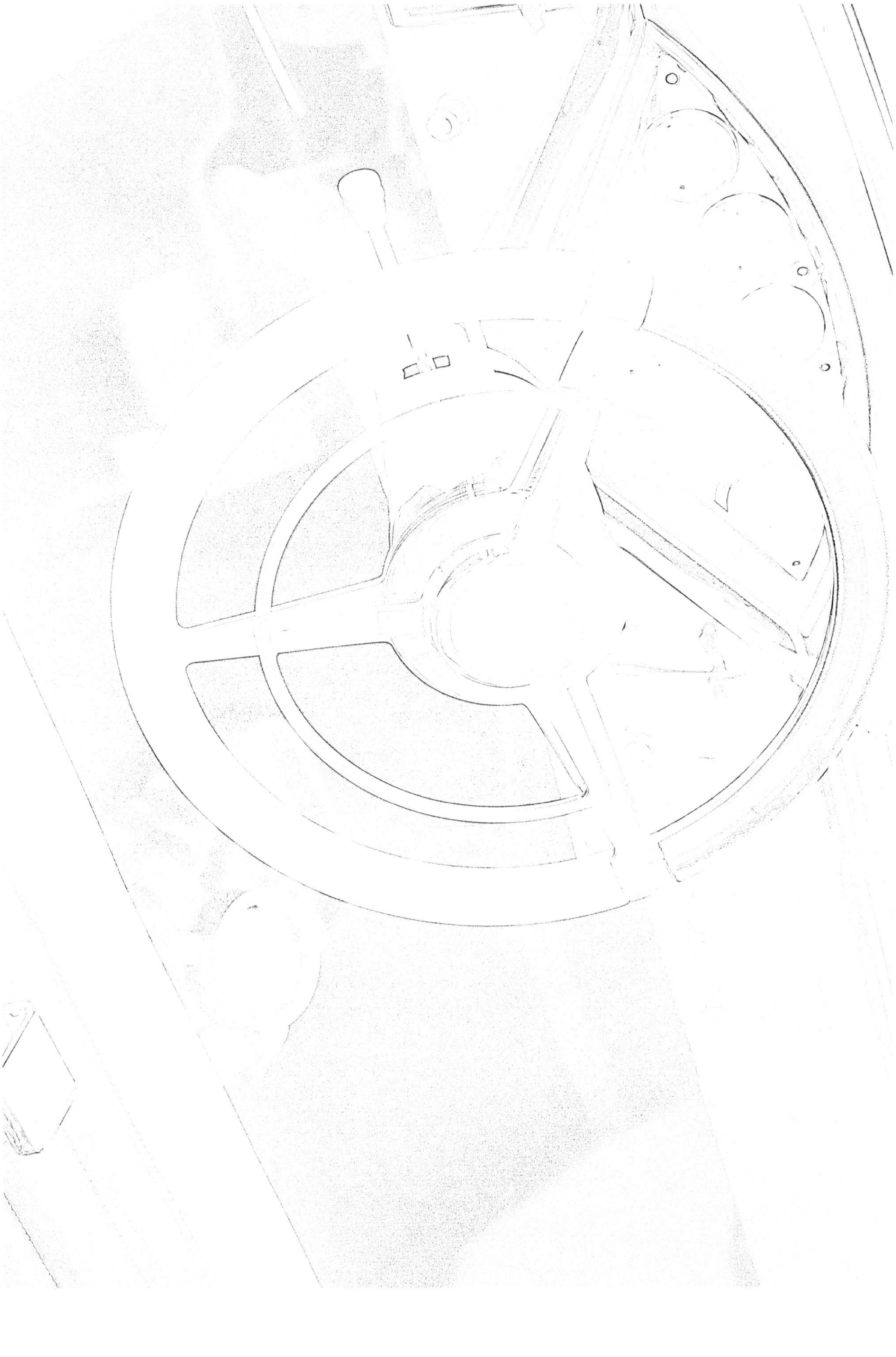

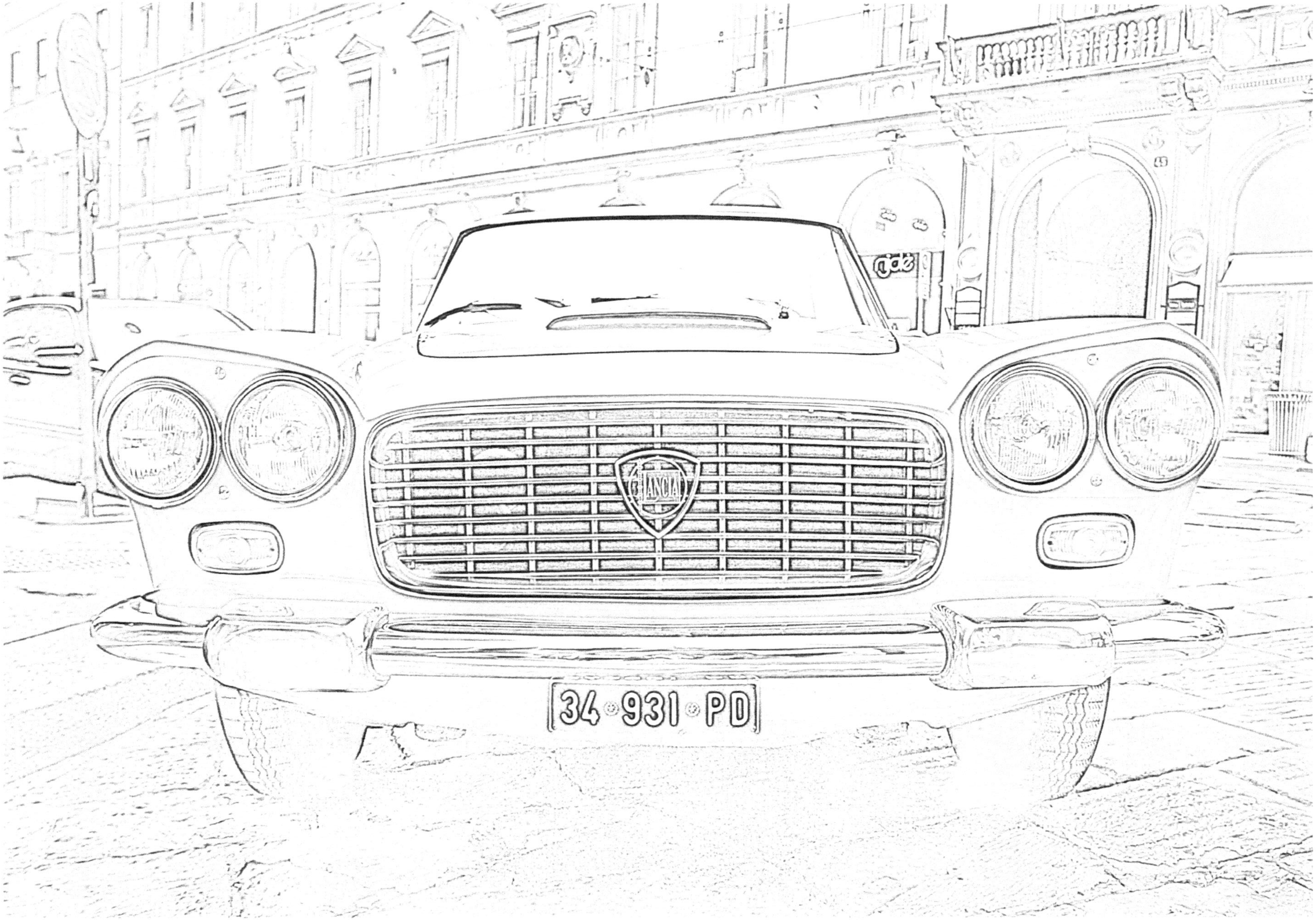
34 931 PD
LANCIA

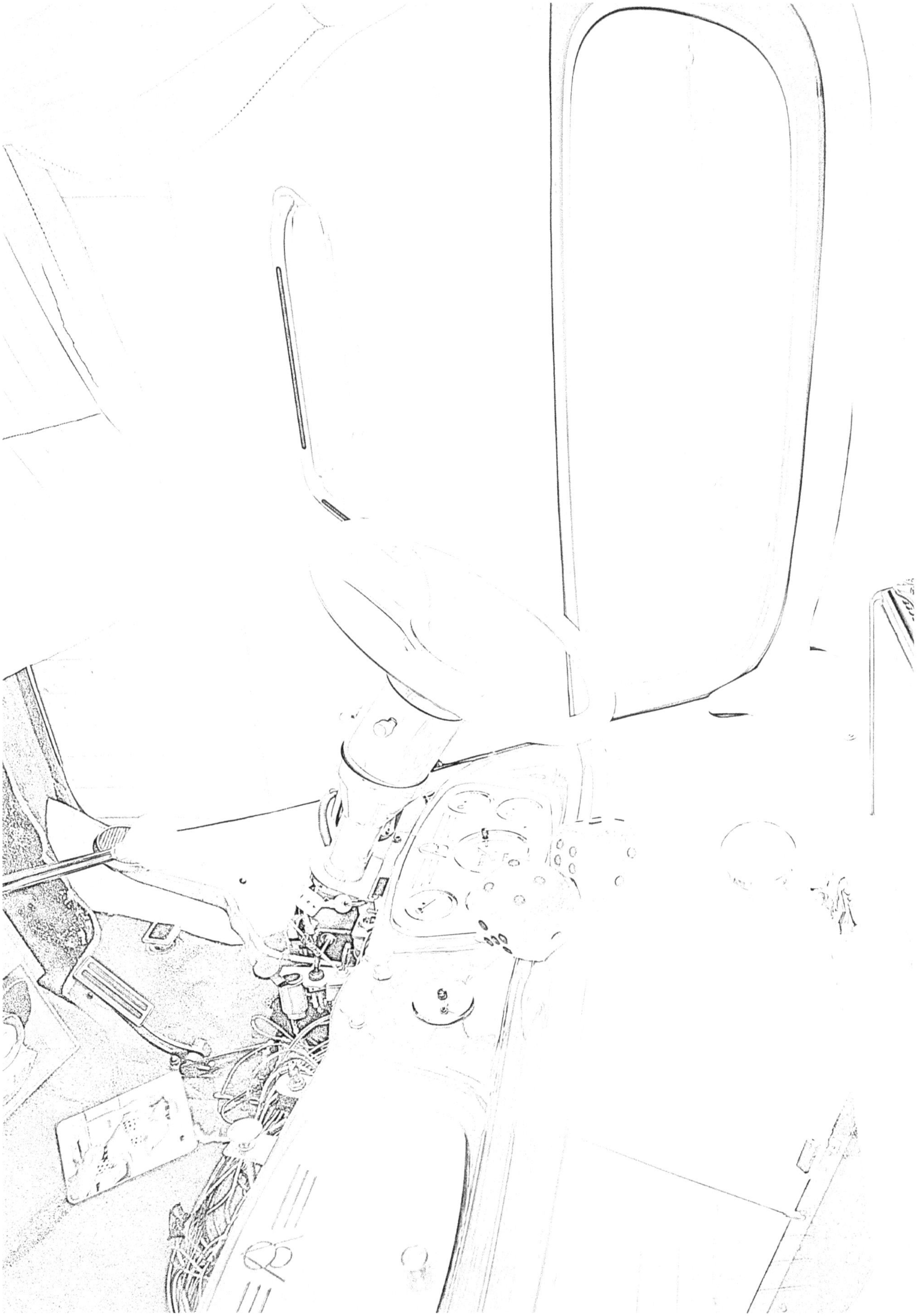

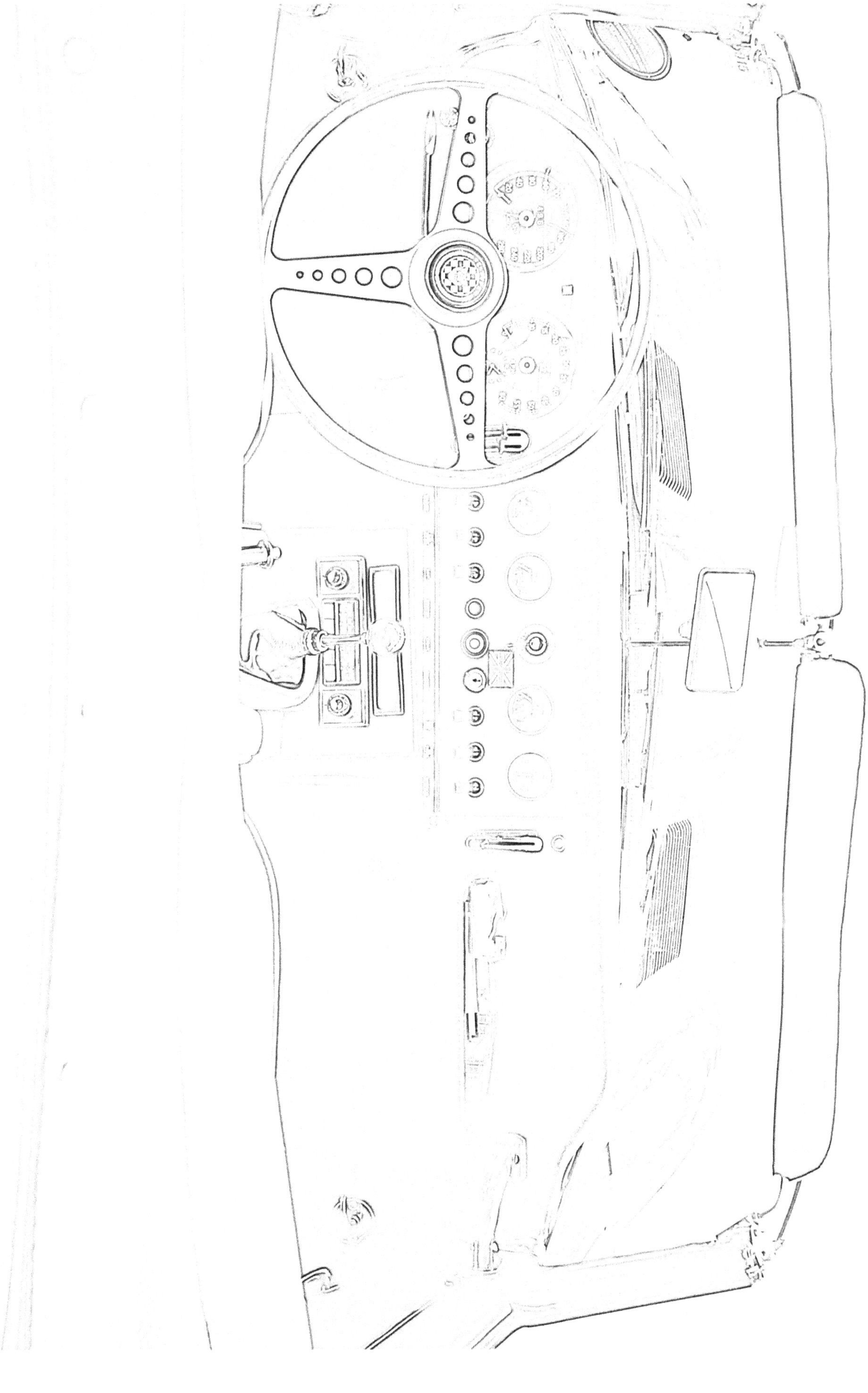

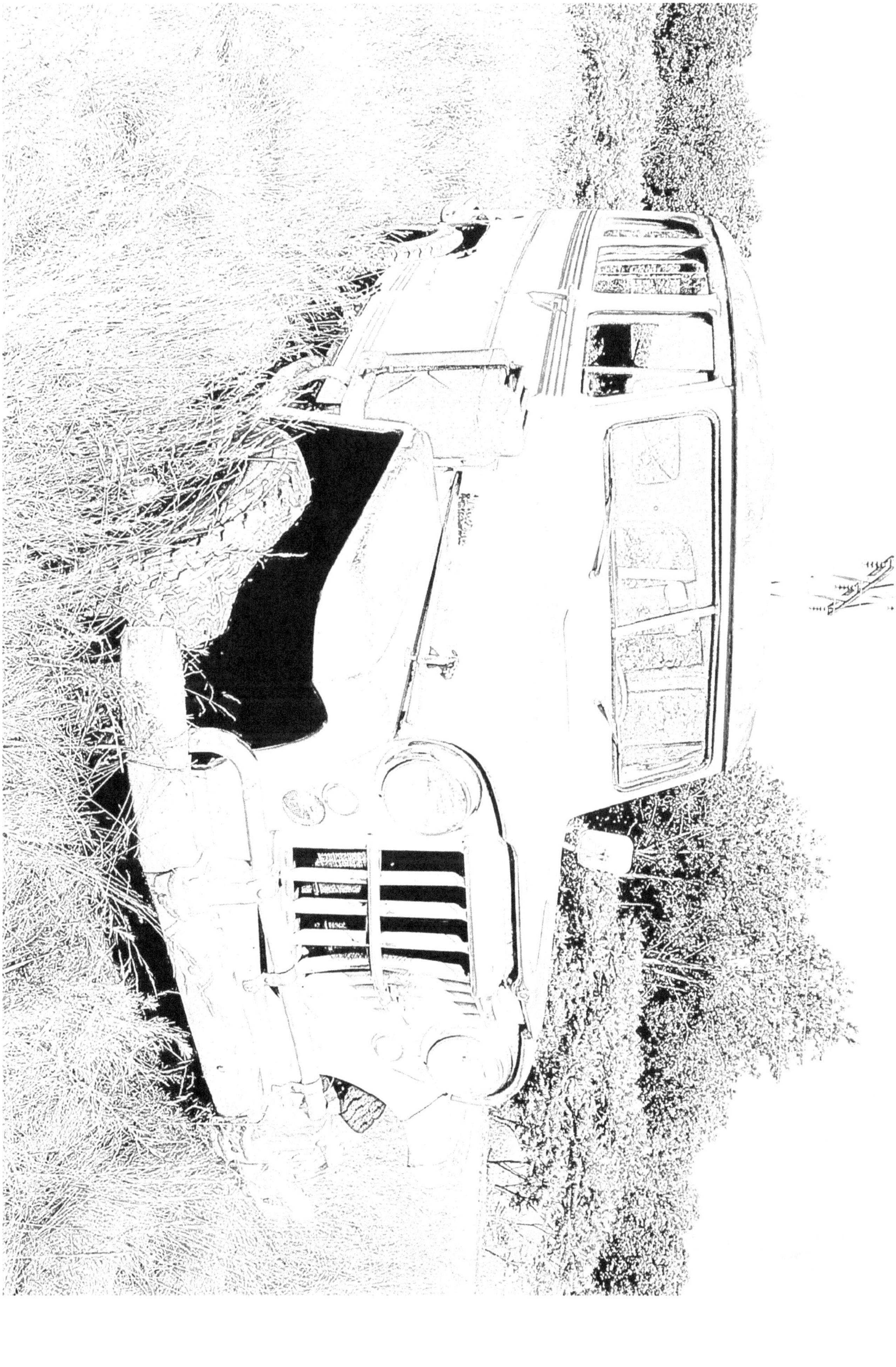

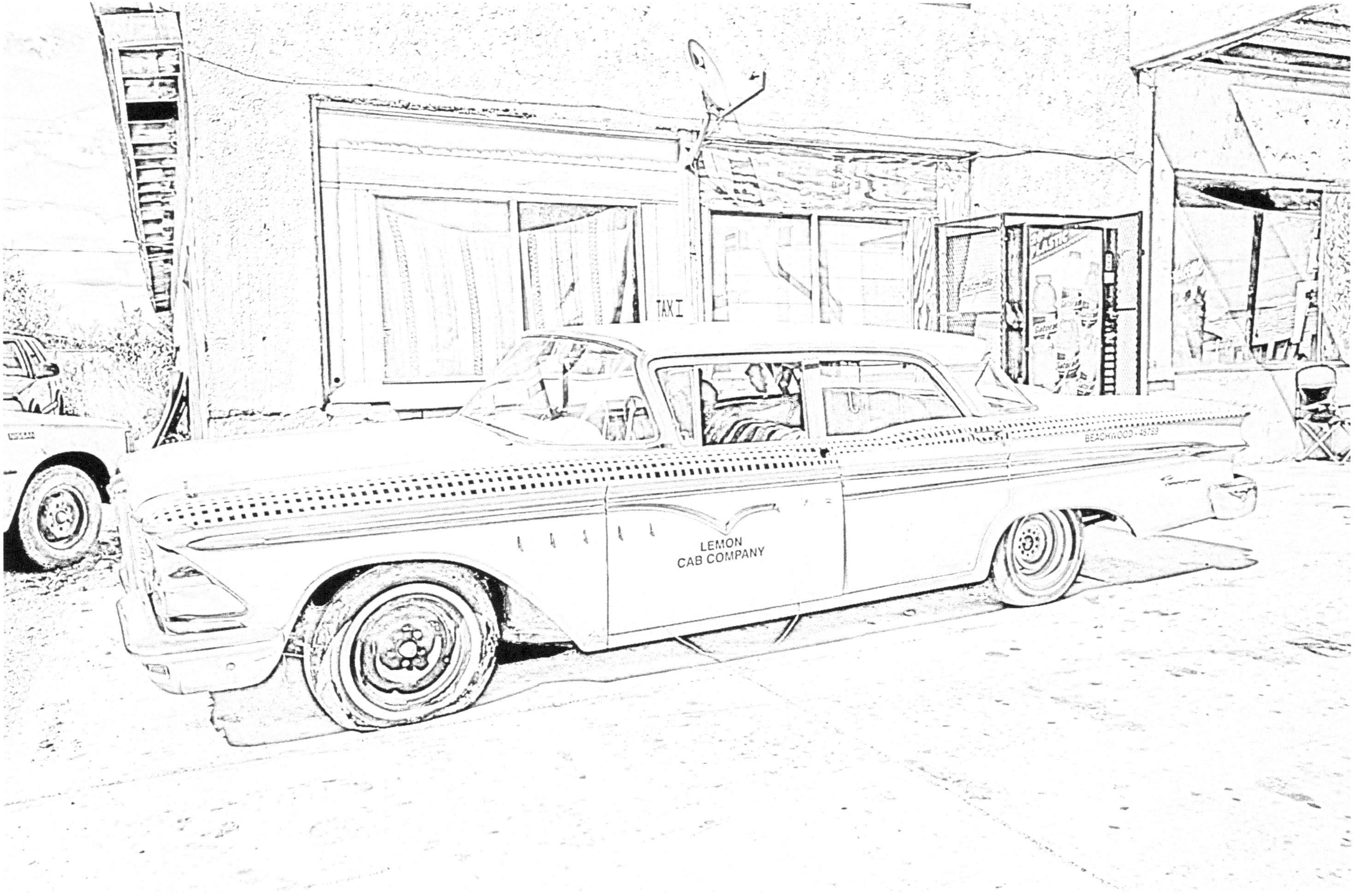
TAXI
LEMON
CAB COMPANY
BEACHWOOD - 45789

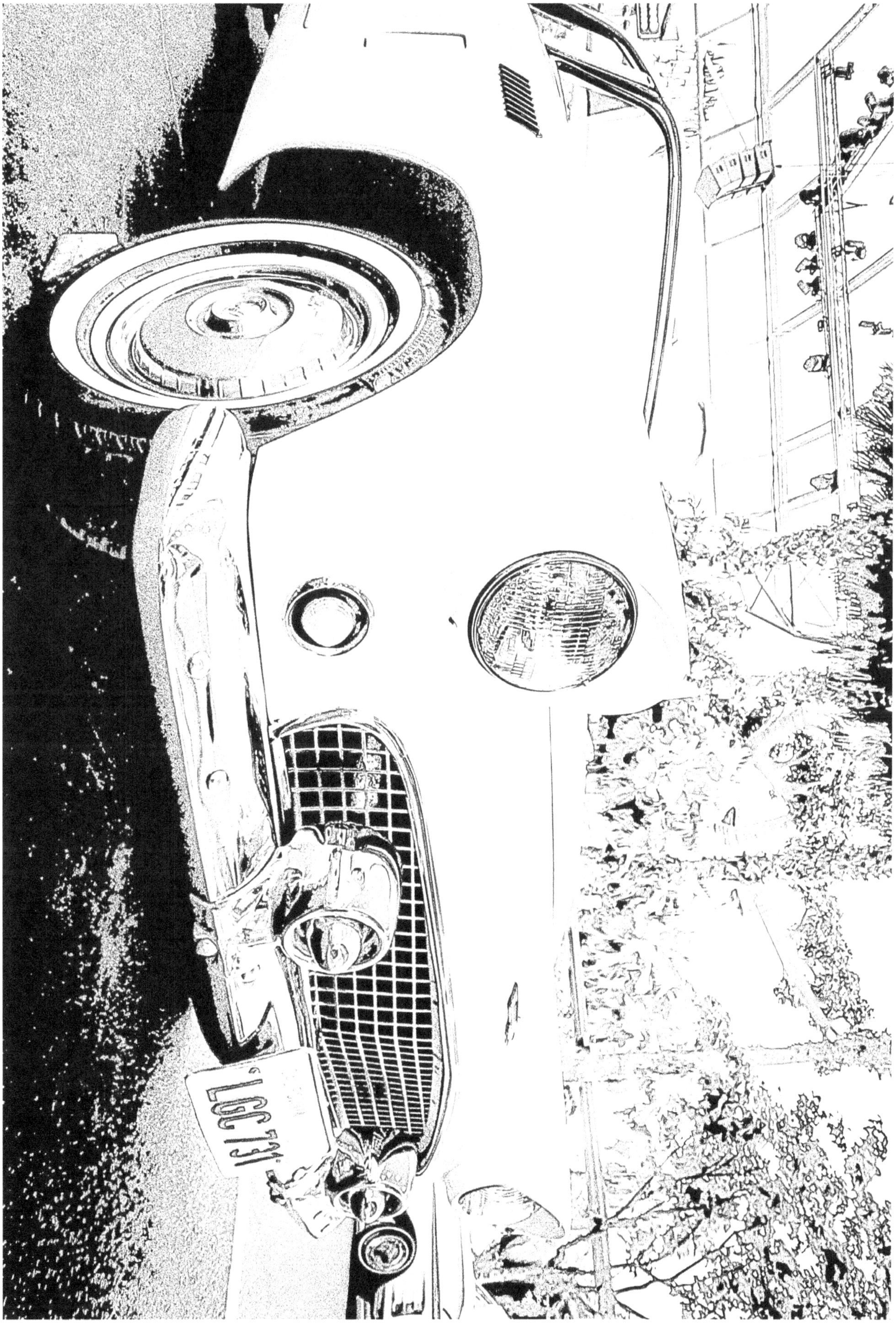
LGC 731

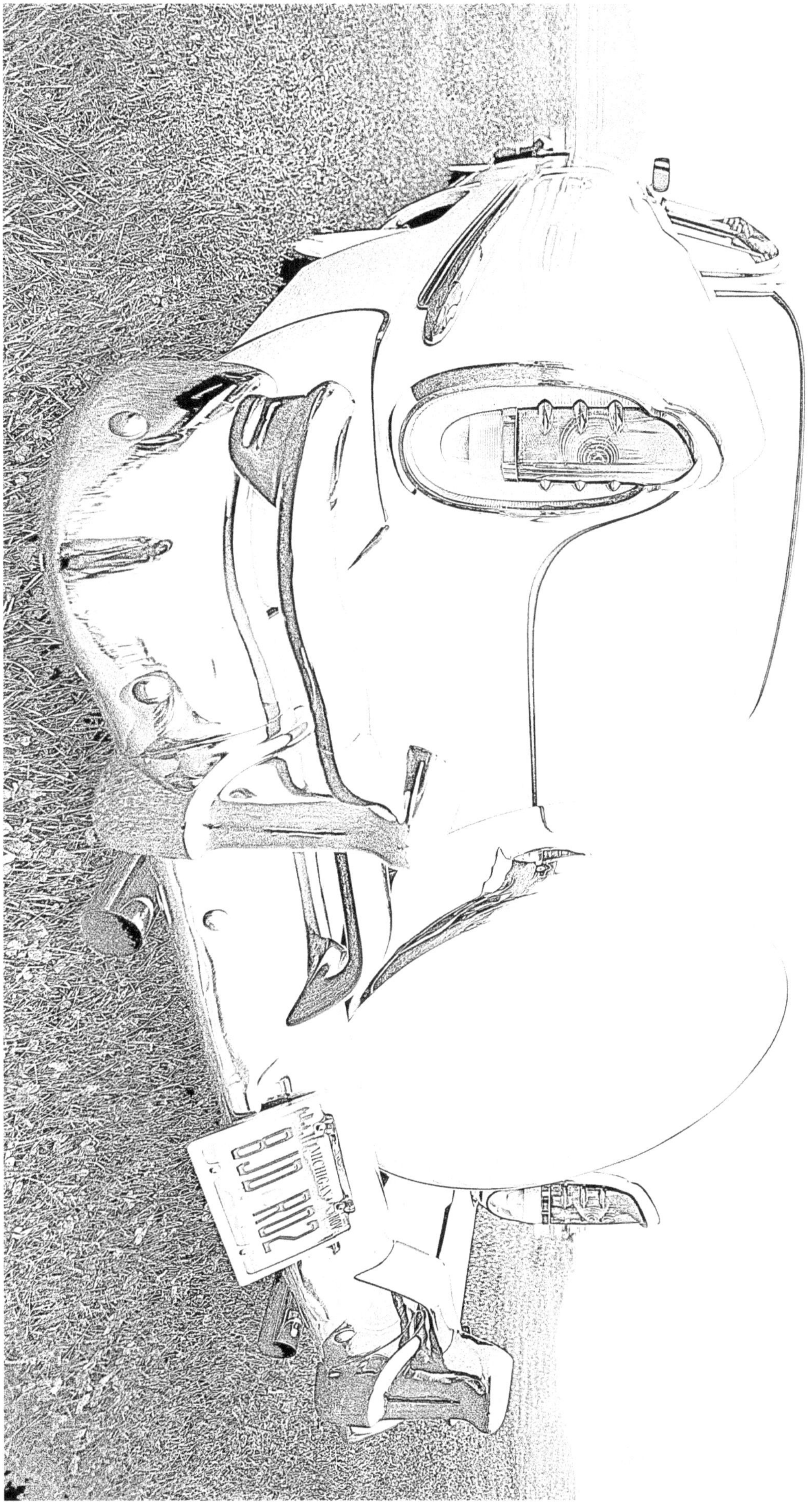

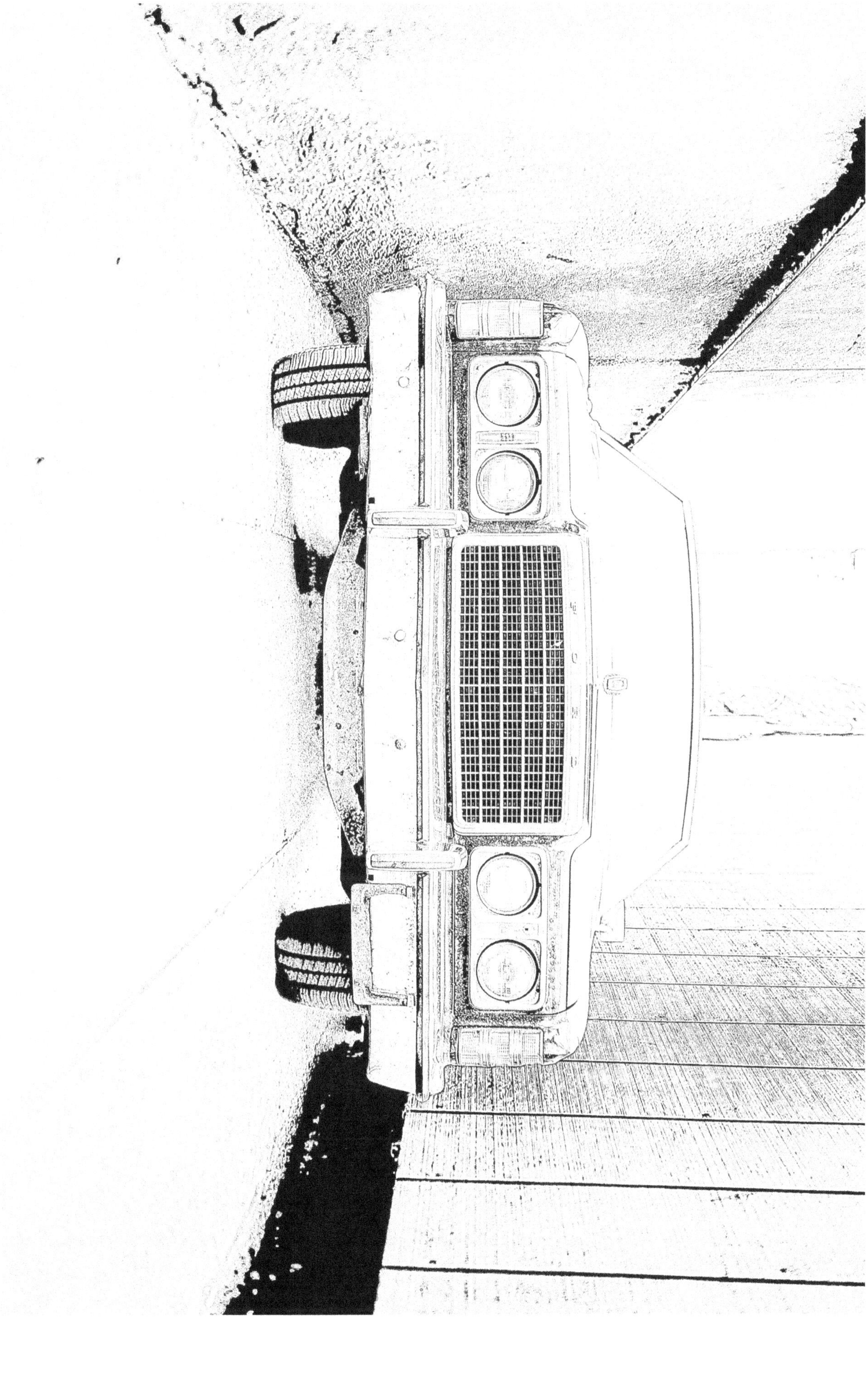

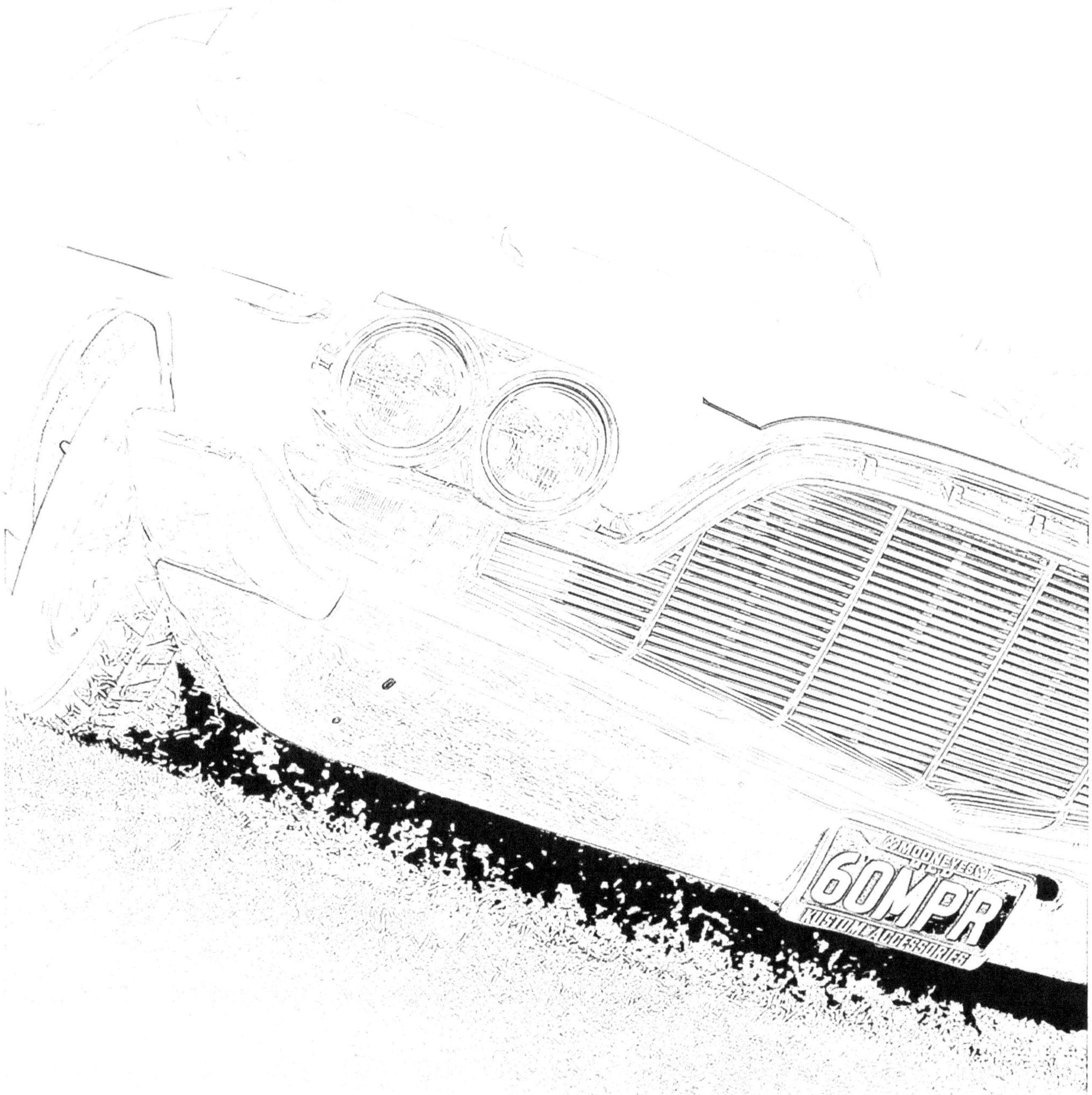
MOONEYES
60MPR
KUSTOM ACCESSORIES

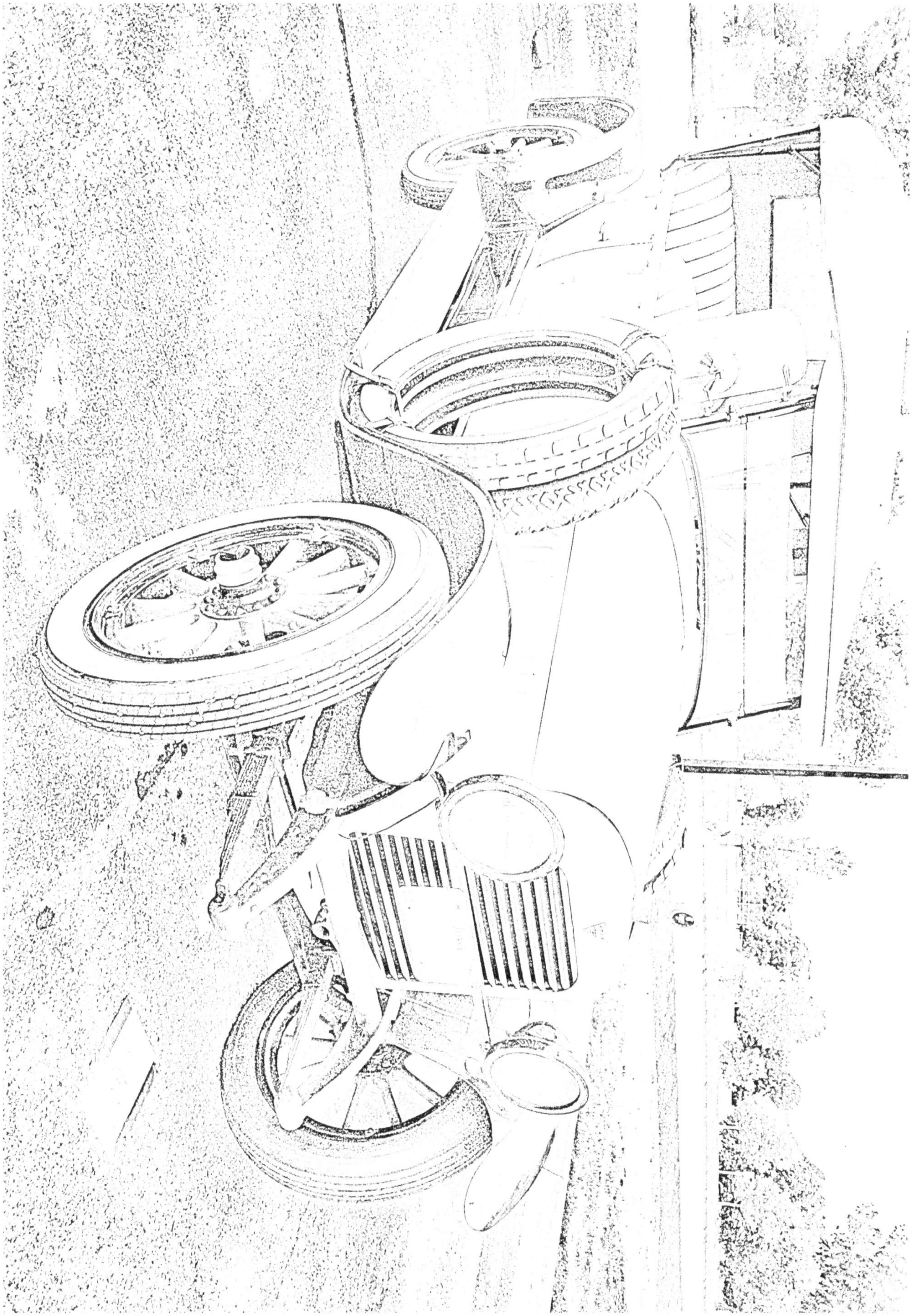

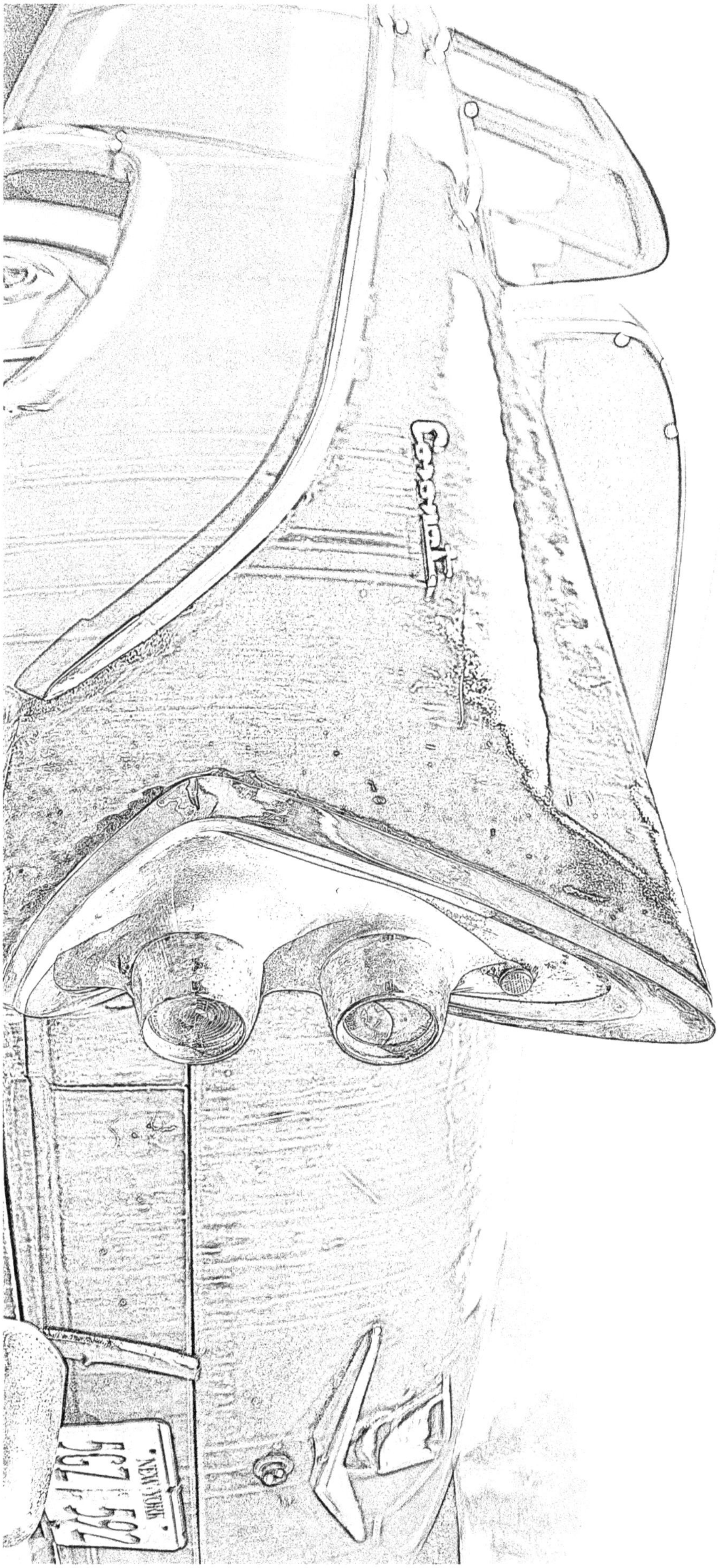

www.ingramcontent.com/pod-product-compliance
Lightning Source LLC
Chambersburg PA
CBHW080830180526
45168CB00006B/2641
* 9 7 8 1 5 1 7 0 1 2 0 4 5 *